Do You See What I See?

DENISE DAVIS

© 2022 by Denise C. Davis

All rights reserved. Except as permitted under the U.S. Copyright Act of 1976, no part of this publication may be reproduced, distributed, or transmitted in any form or by any means, or stored in a database or retrieval system, without the prior written permission of the publisher.

Published by Cleansing the Church Ministries
Post Office Box 534
Hampton, Illinois 61256 U.S.A.

All rights reserved. International copyright secured.

The persons portrayed in this book are composites of different individuals, with most names and some characteristics changed so that the confidentiality of each is completely protected.

Unless otherwise specified, all Scripture quotations in this publication are from the New King James Version. Copyright @ 1979, 1980, 1982, Thomas Nelson, Inc.

Library of Congress Cataloging-in-Publication Data
Davis, Denise C.
    Do You See What I See? / Denise C. Davis.
    Includes bibliographical references.

ISBN 978-1-931845-04-5
      978-1-931845-00-7

Printed in the United States of America

To Timothy

Contents

Prologue: Hi, My Name Is Denise And I'm A Seer ... 5

PART 1 – ANGELS AND DEMONS

1. My Own Personal Dragon ... 11
2. Angels Amongst Us ... 17
3. Demented Demons ... 26
4. Facing the Darkness ... 36
5. Debriefing the Demonic in the Dorm Room ... 44

PART 2 – UNCLEAN SPIRITS

6. My Soul to Keep ... 57
7. Ties That Bind ... 63
8. The Underworld ... 70
9. The Unrest of the Undead ... 80

PART 3 – SOUL TIES

10. When Innocence Expires ... 95
11. Dissever My Soul ... 100

PART 4 – NEPHILIM

12. The Secret Garden ... 109
13. Giants In the Land ... 113

PART 5 – AUTHORITY & SUBJECTION

14.	Spirit Voices	123
15.	Order In Chaos	130
16.	Kingdom of Darkness Chain of Command	136

PART 6 – TO BE ABSENT FROM THE BODY

17.	A Celebration of Death	147
18.	A Solitary Act	150

PART 7 – FREEDOM FROM THE TORMENTORS

19.	Who Shall Separate Us?	161
20.	Weapons of Warfare	168
21.	Let's Break Some Soul Ties!	180
22.	Casting Out Nephilim	184
23.	Freedom From Unclean Spirits	186
	Epilogue: My Secret Is Out!	190

ACKNOWLEDGMENTS	195
APPENDIX I: BIBLES THAT NAME ARCHANGELS	197
APPENDIX II: NAMES OF ARCHANGELS	200
APPENDIX III: THE GREEK GOD PAN	202
NOTES	205
ABOUT THE AUTHOR	215

Do You See What I See?

DENISE DAVIS

PROLOGUE

Hi, My Name Is Denise And I'm A Seer

In those days, if people wanted a message from God, they would say, "Let's go and ask the seer," for prophets used to be called seers.
1 Samuel 9:9

I am a seer. Ghosts' pleas for help and demons' intimidating growls catch my attention. Their scents are as distinguishable as the aroma of brewed coffee or fresh-baked brownies. A spirit's touch is sometimes a breath-on-my-cheek sensation that bristles my neck hair. I do not seek out the spiritual realm; it simply "happens" around us, just as the physical realm does. I have experienced this all of my life. However, I did not consider it a gift from God.

Raised in a devoutly Christian family, I was taught that God exists as three in one[1]—Father, Son, Holy Spirit—and the angels work for them. Satan and his demons torment only deeply disturbed and, most importantly, *deserving* individuals. Additionally, Heaven and Hell exist, and upon our death, every person will go to one of those places. I was taught that our actions determine where we spend eternity, which should be our primary concern. I was sure I would go to Hell because of the hideous spirits I saw. The problem was that some of the Church's teachings about the spirit world clashed with what I saw and experienced.

Whenever I tried to talk to someone about my torment, a devilish spirit quickly reminded me that it would kill whomever I confided in. This tactic was effective, especially when the spirit specifically named my parents. As a child, I had no idea if a demon could or could not kill someone I loved, so I kept my dreadful secret. I tried to be normal, but as time passed, I understood I was different from everyone I knew.

For fear of retaliation, I spent the first two decades of my life talking to nearly no one about the spirit world I saw, heard, and felt. I was twenty-three years old when my first child was born. Three years later, an incident occurred that was so significant that it motivated me to break my silence. One afternoon, I found my son staring intently at a doorway and squealing, *"Dutchy!"* the name of our German Shepherd. Wondering how in the world she managed to get into the house, I looked in the direction he pointed, and sitting there, calm as can be, was a sizable doglike demon. My worst fears were realized—*the seer curse had not ended with me*. I determined that my son would not be tormented as I was and would devote any time and energy needed to ensure it.

Since then, I have invested over thirty years studying the spirit world and drawing conclusions about it by observance, studying biblical spiritual laws, and talking with people about their encounters. I have extensive experience aiding troubled souls in ridding themselves of tormenting spirits. This includes performing exorcisms/cleansings and inner soul healing. What I've written about is what I've learned so far.

I have been dubbed clairvoyant (clear-sighted), clairsentient (clear sensing/feeling), clairaudient (clear hearing), clairalient (clear smelling), and claircognizant (clear knowing). But I am not a psychic or a medium. I do not channel spirits, summon spirit guides, give psychic readings, or practice psychic exercises to increase my so-called powers. I don't worship Satan, perform witchcraft or mind taps, nor call up the dead. I do not read Tarot cards—I don't even read a horoscope. I am a born-again Christian and owe my life entirely to Jesus. If it weren't for His sacrifice and power to free me, I would have perished long ago.

Over time, societies have developed many different and sometimes bizarre theories about the spirit world. Various religions have tried to define this topic.

Today, there are so many versions of the truth that many people wonder whether a spirit world even exists; and if it does, what is it all about?

Some people believe that no spirit world exists and that we are alone on this planet. Others concede there is a spirit world, but no such things as evil spirits, or maybe they are not so much *evil* as they are simply angry. Still, some believe in good spirits and might even call them angels, fairies, or muses.

I have observed that what we believe or do not believe has no bearing on what exists. I am not referring to religion, tradition, or faith. But if we close our eyes, it does not change the scenery before us; we have simply chosen not to see it. Now, there is a big push for scientific proof of spiritual existence. Even with the help of thermal imaging cameras and magnetic readers, there is no scientific proof of a spirit world. But, it is in good company with a few other things whose existence cannot be scientifically proven, such as the human soul: feelings, thoughts, and will. If we base proof of existence on the human ability to see it physically, how do we know the wind exists? The obvious answer is that we see and feel its *effects*: treetops sway, curtains flutter, and leaves and debris dance in perfect rhythm. These inanimate objects move under the wind's influence, proving it exists.

If you can see what I see, you *know* there is a spiritual realm. Oxygen-breathing creatures are not the only entities occupying this planet. Maybe you don't see them, but you see and feel their influence on you and others. Have you ever entered a room, and though there wasn't another living soul in it, you were aware that someone or something else was present? It is possible it was your imagination—it is probable you weren't alone.

So, what types of spirits inhabit the spiritual atmosphere of our world? The spiritual realm is just as diverse as the physical realm. There is great variety in the animal kingdom and humankind; likewise, there is great variety within the spirit world. At the very least, there are good spirits and evil spirits. Many people who don't follow any organized religion believe that good spirits coexist with us. I frequently see good spirits helping people, and even though you might not have drawn any conclusions on what to call them, from this point forward, I will refer to these benevolent spirits as *angels*.

If you see what I see, you know evil spirits co-exist with us. You may wonder what I mean by evil spirits if you do not see them. They are malevolent supernatural creatures driven by violent hatred. Their all-consuming purpose is to do whatever it takes to destroy relationships, steal happiness and love, and kill anything good in our lives.[2] All we need to do is review history to see the influence evil spirits have had on leaders such as Josef Stalin, Adolf Hitler, and Ayatollah Khomeini, to name a few. To communicate more clearly, I will refer to many of these wicked spirits as demons. However, the kingdom of darkness also functions with Nephilim, therion, unclean spirits, fallen angels, and others.

It sounds like I'm describing a horror film or mythological story. That is why many people today dismiss the concept of a spiritual world. There are great novels and exciting films about them. Of course, everyone knows the makings of a good fairy tale include a healthy dose of good versus evil. Without a villain, you can have no hero, right? No wonder it is difficult to believe there is a spirit world. We have trivialized it so dramatically that a thinking person has trouble lending credibility to it—unless you can see it.

Do *you* see what I see? Maybe some of the things I have experienced have also happened to you. Perhaps you try to ignore your spiritual encounters; the last thing you want to do is talk about them. Well, that is precisely what I want to do—*talk about them.*

If you do not see the spirit realm, would you allow my eyes to be your lenses into it? Are you interested in learning how spiritual creatures look and what they can or cannot do? If so, I will give you an eyewitness account of the incredible variety of beings coexisting with us.

Through telling my story, I desire to expose the hidden secrets and treasures of darkness.[3] I will share my encounters with the spirit world and offer you my understanding of it. Do laws of conduct bind this invisible realm? If so, what are they? How do these laws affect human beings?

I invite you to join me on a journey to prove that spiritual laws do indeed apply to the spirit world and that we do not have to remain helplessly controlled by the darkness. My hope is that the eyes of your understanding will be opened to uncover the mysteries of the spirit world.[4]

PART 1

Angels & Demons

CHAPTER ONE

My Own Personal Dragon

The walls are pale yellow. There is no teddy bear wallpaper, balloon or kitten drawings, or any such attempt to give the appearance that the hospital room is intended for a child. One window, with no view to speak of, is positioned off-center on the wall facing the door. The window's flannel-lined vinyl curtains are either intentionally beige or once white but now dingy from years of preventing sunlight from warming the cold room. It feels large, cheerless, and lonely.

An overstuffed nurse with two-tone mustard-gray hair ratted up tight wheels me into the yellow room where I will reside for the next week. Two identical beds resembling oversized baby cribs stand side by side against one wall; mine is the one closest to the door, and the other is empty. I feel somewhat relieved to be closer to the door in case I need to escape.

There are some things I like about this bed right off the bat! It has rails on both sides, the mattress folds up and down at the head end, and the best part is that it's so tall that the bottom comes up to my nose. It is nothing like my bed at home!

The nurse opens a tall metal cabinet, rummages through its neatly stacked contents, and selects a tiny hospital gown speckled with baby-blue rocking horses and yellow giraffes. She lays the gown on the bed, shows my mother where to place my clothes after changing, then steps out of the room, promising to return in a few moments. Once my clothes are changed, Mommy lifts me into the special bed.

On my right side is a metal nightstand with a telephone on top, but I cannot reach it. That's all right, though. There is no reason for me to use the phone unless an adult is present to help me, my mother says. This statement intends to put to rest any ideas I might have of calling my grandfather, my favorite person in the world, at all hours of the night. Besides my own, his is the only other phone number stored in my three-year-old memory—755-7211. I try persuading Mommy to agree that it's okay to call Grandpa because of how much he likes talking to me. She explains about the long distance and that she will not be paying any extra charges. Grandpa will visit me later. I'm sure he will be disappointed if I don't call him, but one glance at Mommy's face indicates that the conversation is finished.

To the left of the bed is a metal table with wheels, the kind on which you set meal trays. For now, it holds a Styrofoam water pitcher and a plastic cup. When the plump nurse returns, she fills the pitcher with ice water and announces, as if it's some kind of party favor, that it is mine to take home once I'm better.

The nurse points out a button at the end of a long cord plugged in behind my bed. If I press The Button, a nurse will immediately come to see me—yes, even in the middle of the night. If I need to use the bathroom, I should press The Button. If I need another blanket, I should press The Button. If I need more ice water, I should press The Button. Later that afternoon, I learn that, apparently, you should *not* press The Button to ask the nurse to change the television channel. That's what the gadget at the end of the other cord plugged in behind my bed is for. But really, the plump nurse should have mentioned that in her "Button" speech at the beginning. Then she would not have had to traipse all the way down the long hallway just to explain that to me, what with her sore feet and all.

Next, the nurse displays the bed's most fantastic attribute—the *see-through tent*. At home, I love to play tent! One bed sheet can transform almost anything into a tent: four chairs, two couches, a swing set, and my father's pool table. But, *my bed* is the most desirable object of all to make into a tent. However, this is strictly prohibited as I am not allowed to put chairs with dirty feet in the middle of the mattress. So, this tent bed is nearly a dream come true!

Once she smooths down the plastic tent sides, the nurse turns on a machine that begins purring a cool mist inside. She explains that the mist will help me breathe, so I should stay inside the tent at all times. That morning Dr. Keen told my mother the reason I couldn't breathe was because of the pneumonia. I suppose the pneumonia gets into your lungs, and its job is to keep the air out. Now the cool mist will go in and push the pneumonia out. The plump nurse says if we have any questions or need anything, we should push The Button, and she will return. But, I have the impression that returning would be quite a bother to her. Then she disappears through the door.

As the clock ticks closer to bedtime, a night shift nurse steps halfway into my room and asks my mother if she is staying the night. She says that she is. Well then, the nurse says, she will have to be sleeping in the chair because they don't bring in cots. Mommy says she doesn't mind. She will be quite comfortable if she can only have a pillow and a blanket. Looking clearly put out and prune-faced about it, the nurse disappears for a few minutes and then reappears with the requested pillow and blanket.

The pink vinyl chair doesn't look comfortable. Here I am in a cozy tent bed, and Mommy will be scrunched into a small chair with only a blanket and a pillow. Swayed by my empathy for my mother's discomfort, I tell her it will be all right if she goes home. However, this is a bald-faced lie as I do not in any way wish to be left alone in my sterile room under the care of the unfriendly nurses. Still, I say it is only for tonight, and will she promise to be back first thing tomorrow morning…maybe even before I wake up? Not accepting this offer, she asks how I would feel if I woke up alone in the night? I lie again. I assure her I will be fine, though I don't feel as sure as I try to sound. My parents naturally suppose my nightly requests for stories, drinks of water, and lullabies are my way of extending the bedtime hour; they are nothing of the sort. You see, I have a secret I must keep, and my greatest fear is that somebody will discover it.

I *dread* being alone in the dark, but that's not my secret. It's not the dark that I fear. I am terrified of what's *in it!* And what's in it is the creature silently squatting against the wall near the lone window. Now, after the second lie, it leisurely disentangles its webbed forelimbs while rising upon its haunches. Oh, how I hate it when Beastie moves! The scaly arms grate against its leathery sides as it exhales a deep smoky hiss. Gray vapor circles the nearly footlong pointed horns on the sides of its head, then floats into the atmosphere. The ceiling is not high enough for the creature to stand completely erect, causing its shoulders to hunch and the head to thrust forward and down. Now, the corners of its mouth begin to turn upward in quiet approval of these fortunate circumstances.

Also worth fearing in the dark is the tall man standing in the corner of the room opposite the creature. Though there is kindness in his eyes, he is clearly *not* human. For starters, his clothing is not separate from his body. His boots *are* his feet, his helmet *is* the top of his head, and his vest *is* his chest. Though he has never approached me, I don't feel at ease in his presence simply because of his massive size; his head is clearly above the door jam. Now the tall man takes one giant step closer to my bed, maneuvering himself between Beastie and me. Keeping his eyes fixed on the creature, he places his hand at his side where a sheathed golden rapier-type knife rests; he silently pats it.

"You know I have the right to be here," the beast fires at the tall man. "I've bode time sixty years in wait for her. You know the Law: I have the license to pursue as far as the third and fourth generations.[1] You can't prevent me from moving into where I am invited. She *lied*," wheezing out the last word for emphasis.

These two, the beast and the tall man, have always attended my way, but this is the first time I ever heard Beastie speak. At the end of life, every creature makes a gurgling sound as the lungs fill with fluid and it releases its last breath. The voice of the beast was this death rattle. I will never forget it.

I don't understand any of this "Law" talk and wonder why the man is silent.

The creature plods closer—click-click, click-click—its needle claws scrape the old linoleum floor. The stench of its breath reaches across fifteen feet of the room and seeps under the tent. Like a punch in the gut, I instantly realize the tent will not protect me, and this bed is no different from my bed at home.

I don't remember moving into my big girl bed. I also cannot recall the beginning of the beast creature bothering me at night; it was always present. At first, it sat in the shadow of my dresser, breathing its hissy fumes. I couldn't see it clearly, but it made sure I knew it was there. When the fear became intolerable, I would cry to Mommy that I was thirsty (my go-to rescue plea). But as it does in thousands of homes with toddlers, this scenario always played out the same way. "Go back to sleep! You already had enough water, and there is nothing in your closet or under your bed! That's your imagination." I did not understand how my "imagination" pulled me by my legs out of bed and onto the cold tile floor. Or why, even with blankets covering my head, my imagination clutched my throat and squeezed until I could barely breathe.

Until now, Beastie hadn't actually approached me. It didn't need to because it simply ordered the more minor tormenting spirits to pinch, squeeze, or nip at my fingers. But since that fateful lie to my mother, the creature now skulks toward the bed, squinty eyes fixed on the tall man, occasionally flashing a glance in my direction. Why is it coming closer? How does it know I lied? As it moves ever nearer, I look at the tall man with pleading eyes. *Why doesn't he make it go away?* But, the tall man doesn't move, doesn't speak, doesn't intervene.

This fleeting look stops the creature in its tracks, and it stares directly at me. My palms begin sweating with nervousness, and I look to the man for reassurance. Instantly, the beast appears startled, and its yellow pupils rapidly dilate and contract. It focuses closely on my face as the room falls silent for a dozen uncomfortable seconds. Then an amused expression dawns on Beastie's hideous face, and the terrifying creature speaks directly to me for the first time in my short life. "You…can…*see*…me?" its voice drags over each word. With all the confidence of a matador entering an arena, it straightens up and victoriously stabs, "You *can* see me!" This statement knocks the wind right out of me.

Soon there is no distance between the beast and my fortress. Without disturbing the plastic tent, it crawls up under it. I am exposed and frozen with fear! The great creature takes its time cozying up on the foot of the bed, and after many lengthy seconds, it whispers, "If you so much as breathe one word about me to any living creature, I will kill your mother first, then your father, and your sniveling sister last. Then pathetic little you will be all alone. Because no one wants a child like you." As the weight of these words hit my chest, I squeeze my eyes shut and sing a Sunday School song in my head, *O be careful little eyes what you see…O be careful little eyes what you see. For the Father up above is looking down in love so, be careful little eyes what you see.* I am convinced I am evil because I see evil.

The English writer G.K. Chesterton put it best, "Fairy tales do not tell children that dragons exist. Children already know that dragons exist. Fairy tales tell children that dragons can be killed." My mother tells me she slept in the pink vinyl chair all night, but my terrified little girl memory concluded she had left. Huddled in that hospital bed in the dreary yellow room, I felt truly alone. Because at that moment, I realized my own personal dragon could not be killed.

CHAPTER TWO

Angels Amongst Us

Angels descending, bring from above,
Echoes of mercy, whispers of love.
Fanny J. Crosby, "Blessed Assurance"

Can angels really help us? Can demons actually harm us? By the time I was an adult, I questioned if the spirit world had *any* rules because it seemed to me that the beast and his demons had no boundaries, freely tormenting me night and day. Hollywood provides us with creative and often far-fetched ideas of angels and demons, but I have noticed that what I see does not line up with some of their fantastical descriptions.

The topic of angels is *vast*. We can trace the idea of their existence throughout antiquity in societies, religions, and philosophies. There are thousands of books, essays, theses, blogs, and websites written about them, and the small portion of this book designated to this subject is by no means exhaustive. A quick disclaimer: I mentioned in the Prologue that I am a Christian, so many of my explanations in this book will be about how that has helped, guided, and saved me from the kingdom of darkness. If you're not yet ready, feel free to skip these, but I hope to share my experiences with you. Nevertheless, you might find it interesting that over the past ten or fifteen years, we've delivered extremely tormented people of high-ranking spirits that go by the names of some so-called Archangels listed in various bibles and sacred texts.[1]

I have learned that not all bibles are created equal, nor were they intended to be. What each of them has in common, thereby dividing them, is that followers believe their bible is the final authority. But, the greatest test of authority is whether or not a spiritual entity is affected by it. The true Word of God is not simply a historical storybook. It's a supernatural book alive with spiritual laws, and the unseen world has no option but to abide by them. There is only one God-breathed book; if the others don't measure up to that one, they are merely interesting reading material. I wholeheartedly trust the Christian Bible because I've seen it in action. Its laws are the only ones that actually affect the kingdom of darkness. So, I will use text from that bible in my explanations.

That being said, here are some questions about angels I am often asked.

What are angels?

The word angel means *a messenger dispatched as a deputy*.[2] Angels are spirit beings created by God and authorized as His representatives to act on His behalf. Long before humans entered the scene, there was a season of time when angels had free will, and they could choose to serve God or not. In essence, free will allows a being to make choices without coercion or force. If a being does not have free will, an outside force controls their actions. So for an unknown period, all of the angels chose to be loyal to God and serve Him through the ranks and jobs they were created for.

This brings us to Lucifer, the great leader of the angelic rebellion. Technically, he was not an angel. Lucifer was a cherub, which is a different type of celestial being. He was the highest-ranked cherub with the title of "the anointed cherub who covers the mountain of God."[3] Cherubim were (and still are) guardians of God's heavenly throne. The name Lucifer means *Light-bearer*, and his name described his abilities.[4] Next to Jesus, who *is* the Light,[5] Lucifer was probably physically closest to the throne of God.

One day, Lucifer decided to exercise his free will as he shook his fist in his Creator's face and said:

1. I will ascend into Heaven.

2. I will exalt my throne above the stars of God.

3. I will also sit on the mount of the congregation on the farthest sides of the north.

4. I will ascend above the heights of the clouds.

5. I will be like the Most High.[6]

What did these declarations mean? They were a slap to the face of Jehovah and a direct rebellion against His authority. The short story is that the sum of these "I wills" meant Lucifer was finished with bringing glory to God and decided to keep it for himself. So, during this season of angelic free will, Lucifer managed to get himself and a third of the angels cast out of Heaven to the Earth.[7] This event abruptly ended the season of angelic free will. From then on, angels who remained loyal to God served Him exclusively. The angels thrown out of Heaven with Lucifer now serve him *on our planet*. How lucky are we!

From the days of mankind's life in the garden of Eden, we have known of the existence of angels. God created Adam and Eve with free will to choose to serve God or themselves, just as Lucifer once did. We've all heard how the story goes. They chose to eat from the tree of knowledge of good and evil, the only thing God told them never to do.[8] So God sent Adam and Eve out of the garden, and He placed cherubim on the east side to guard the way to the tree of life.[9]

King David wrote in Psalms 91:11, "For He (Jehovah) will order His angels to protect you wherever you go." And in Psalm 103:20, David also wrote, "Bless the Lord, you His angels, you mighty ones who do His commandments, hearkening to the voice of His word."

We see belief in the help of angels in many other societies and writings other than the Christian Bible. When telling the story of Socrates' death, Plato describes how God sends a spirit to guide and guard individuals through the dying process, a common concept in ancient Greek philosophy.[10]

Muslims honor angels as an essential part of their faith. The Quran declares that its message was communicated verse by verse through an angel.

They believe the angel Gabriel revealed the Quran to the prophet Muhammad and communicated with all other prophets.[11]

Hindus, Buddhists, and Theosophists call supernatural beings similar to angels *devas*. Still, some folks who do not believe in God or any being of a higher level believe that aliens or otherworldly creatures coexist with us to watch over and protect humankind.

Why do angels look different from other spirit beings?

Thanks to Renaissance-era artists, the idea of angels conjures images of white-winged, halo-ensconced toddlers flitting about the clouds. Though a romantic notion, I have never seen such creatures. Maybe I should begin by describing what angels do *not* look like. They do not have feathery wings. They do not look like chubby impish children playing harps. They *never* look like naked seductive men or women. They are not here to sexually pleasure humans. I know people who have seen and even had sex with spirits who appeared to them as seductive men or women; however, these spirits are not angels. They are fallen angels or Nephilim. We'll talk more about these creatures later.

Just as people are physically unique, so are angels. In contrast to the animal or reptilian features of demons, most angels appear to have human characteristics with superhuman qualities. For example, I have seen some who were forty feet tall. Angels that interact with people always appear as human men. I have spoken with many people who received help in times of distress from "men" who instantly appeared and disappeared as soon as the helpful deed was accomplished. This means some angels can materialize in physical form.[12] I have seen them in both spirit form and physical form.

What types of angels are there? What do they do?

We are most familiar with the idea of angels guarding and protecting us. But that's not all they do! According to the Bible, angels also can deliver, guide, enlighten or reveal information, provide for believers, serve as instruments of

God's judgments, carry out some of God's answers to our prayers, encourage, strengthen, serve, and help people at their time of death, carrying them to meet their Maker. That last one intrigues me. Because Satan is the ruler of the power of the air, angels protect us as we pass from this world into our heavenly home. I have seen this type of angel many times as they escort spirits from this planet. As you can see, there are several types, or classifications, of angels; their job description depends on their class. Here are some angel types.

Archangels

Archangels are probably the most controversial and troublesome type of angel to clarify. The reason is that there are multitudes of theories about them. Nevertheless, all of these ideas agree on one thing: an archangel is the highest-ranking of all angels.

The Jewish Hebrew Bible (also the Christian Bible's Old Testament) uses the term *angel* (*mal'ak*) 217 times and means *one sent*; however, archangel is never used. This is because archangel is originally a Greek word (*archaggelos*), meaning *chief of angels*. Since the Jewish Bible's original text is Hebrew, archangel would not be included. The book of Daniel 10:13 describes what is commonly interpreted as a spiritual battle between an evil demonic prince and Michael, the first patron angel of all time. After reading the Jewish author Jude's writings (New Testament), many biblical scholars agree that Daniel's chief angel Michael was also Jude's archangel Michael. He said, "Michael the archangel, in contending with the devil, disputed about the body of Moses."[13] In both cases, the Archangel Michael fulfills a warrior role.[14]

There is a growing belief that archangels are here solely to protect and support humans, and we should solicit them by name. But I have a problem with this idea. As of 2020, the world population was slightly more than 7.8 billion. If an archangel is the highest-ranking angel of its kind, limited to one place at a time, and just one of each exists, why would they see fit to visit individual humans whenever we call upon them? Maybe archangels are being confused with *ministering angels*.

Ministering Angels

These angels attend to the needs and comforts of deeply distressed people. They especially frequent hospitals, convalescent homes, and hospice facilities. My grandmother's last days were spent in the hospital as she had suffered a severe stroke; Mom and her sisters kept a twenty-four-hour vigil at Grandma's bedside. Each reported how for days, Grandma drifted in and out of sleep, smiling and humming an unrecognizable tune. Suddenly gesturing toward the ceiling and around the room, she would declare, "Oh! Can you hear them? They're all singing, and it's so beautiful. Listen…can you hear them?" I was not present, though I am confident that a beautiful choir of ministering angels serenaded my grandmother. I have witnessed this scene repeated multiple times in the many cities and countries I have visited.

This type of angel visited Jesus Christ twice when he was deeply distressed.[15] The Book of Mark tells us that the first time this occurred was at the beginning of Jesus' ministry. "And He was there in the wilderness forty days, tempted by Satan, and was with the wild beasts; and *the angels ministered to him*."[16] The second visitation was at the end of his ministry in the Garden of Gethsemane. This is the famous scene depicted in many paintings and sermon illustrations when Jesus prayed, "Father, if it is Your will, take this cup away from me" (referring to his coming crucifixion); "nevertheless not my will, but Yours, be done. Then an angel from heaven appeared to him, *strengthening him*."[17] This means the angel was given power to rejuvenate Jesus in his body and soul. While the prophet Elijah ran for his life from the evil queen Jezebel, he prayed that he might die, begged Jehovah to take his life then fell asleep under a tree. At two different times, a ministering angel awakened him by touch and told him to consume the food and water he provided. After the second time, Elijah "went in the strength of that food forty days and forty nights."[18]

Probably the most popular angel theory is that when people die, they transform into ministering angels to bring messages of love, warning, correction, and instruction to humans. However, for this to be true, humans lose their free will to choose and become controlled subjects of God through the death of the body. Why would God create humans to exercise free will to choose to love him or not and then remove that choice upon death?

Warrior Angels

Another type of angel always involved in spiritual battles against evil spirits I call *warrior angels*. These angels do *not* fight humans however, they do battle the demons that desire to control humans. Warrior angels protect hemispheres, regions, cities, buildings, and people. I will share an exciting story involving warrior angels a few chapters from now.

Guardian Angels

Each person does have their very own angel assigned to them at birth, called a *guardian angel*.[19] Some people have vague memories of seeing their guardian angel when they were little more than toddlers. One friend remembers a "man" standing at the foot of her crib holding "scary creatures" at bay. Dr. Julie Barrier tells this story, "I Met My Daughter's Guardian Angel":

> I heard Roger shout, "Julie, get to the bathtub NOW!!!" There was an unusual urgency in his voice. I dropped the laundry and sprinted toward our sunken tub. We had a large tile sunken tub in the back of the house that was about four feet deep. As I bounded through the bathroom door, little Brie was precariously teetering head-first toward the cement floor.
>
> I scooped my baby up and pressed her tightly to my chest. Roger ran toward us just as I carried her to safety.
>
> "Oh, honey," I sighed. "What would we have done if you hadn't warned me?"
>
> "I didn't call you, Julie," he replied, astonished. "I heard YOU scream, 'Roger, get to the bathroom. Hurry!"
>
> We looked at each other, speechless. Neither one of us had spoken a word of warning, yet we were clearly summoned to avert the disaster.
>
> That was the first time we met Brie's guardian angel. We thanked God for sparing our baby daughter. I was reminded of Psalm 34:7 "The angel of

the Lord encamps around those who fear him, and he delivers them."[20]

Once I watched a homeless man sitting on a sidewalk leaning against a wall. He held his head in his hands and looked pitifully destitute. His guardian angel knelt near him, never leaving his side. The angel cupped his hand by his mouth and spoke closely into the man's ear as a dear friend would. It was intimate, personal, and tender. The angel was careful with him. He held onto the man's arm and attempted to coax him to stand several times. For many moments, the man appeared dismal and despairing. The angel persisted. After much encouragement, the man finally stood to his feet and plodded on while the angel cheered and praised him.

Good, bad, poor, rich, famous, obscure; the only qualifying criterion to have a guardian angel is that one must simply be human. It is essential to understand one of the most important spiritual laws by which this kind of angel must abide: a guardian angel cannot override or change our wills or choices. This means the angel cannot prevent their actions if someone attempts to harm themselves or someone else. They can only speak to the person and try to convince them to do otherwise. I sincerely wish they could do immeasurably more than this.

The English author Clive Barker said, "Superman is, after all, an alien life form. He's simply the acceptable face of invading realities." I believe most folks would like to know they have their own personal Superman who protects them. In a way, guardian angels are alien life forms—good spirits who, like Superman, protect and offer us help.

There are many opinions regarding the role guardian angels play. Whereas an archangel has minimal human contact, guardian angels attend our way from birth to protect us along life's journey. If you can see what I see, then you know each human being, whether religious or not, has at least one angel following them everywhere they go. This is a promise we can hold on to! God says he will order his angels to protect you wherever you go.[20] After reflecting on your life, you may be thinking, "Well, that solves a few mysteries!"

In the hospital story, you'll remember the otherworldly tall man staring down the beastly creature. I understand now that this tall being was my guardian angel. But I didn't have this knowledge for many years. In the meantime, I seriously questioned God as to why he would provide the appearance of help but not allow him to do anything to save me from the beast. This event created a deep wound in my soul and a growing mistrust of God's power and intentions. That was precisely the calculated deception the kingdom of darkness was trying to accomplish through this experience.

Why didn't my guardian angel intervene and fight the demon, comfort me, or speak to me?

It's not that the angel didn't intervene; it's more like he couldn't. *What? You say. Doesn't good always battle evil?* No, it does not, and knights in shining armor sometimes fall off their noble steeds. The reason he couldn't intervene was because of a spiritual law.

I'll explain it this way: if you are a citizen of one country and move to another country, you must abide by the laws governing the country to where you have moved. If you are arrested and jailed in that country, in most cases, your home government cannot intervene on your behalf. When I lied, it was as if I had moved to a foreign country and agreed to live by their laws. The demon governed that country, and my choice prohibited the angel from saving me from my circumstances. The fact that I was a child was irrelevant to the demon.

CHAPTER THREE

Demented Demons

Monsters are real, and ghosts are real too.
They live inside me, and sometimes, they win.
Stephen King

C.S. Lewis said, "There are two equal and opposite errors into which our race can fall about devils (demons). One is to disbelieve in their existence. The other is to believe and to feel an excessive and unhealthy interest in them." I find it remarkable that religions and societies will turn a pacifistic cheek to believing in or discussing angels. But bring up the topic of demons or evil spirits, and suddenly everyone has an opinion worth fighting over.

One school of thought about demons is that the belief in their existence is Christian-based, created by a tyrannical God used as a human control mechanism. The idea is that if people are adequately afraid of demons, then God has the leverage to turn disobedient followers over to them. However, not all Christians believe that demons even exist. Of those who do, the majority suppose Christians are exempt from demonic influence. This theory makes no sense to me because demons follow Christians and non-Christians alike. On the other end of the spectrum, most psychologists consider no one to be spiritually demonized—demons exist only in the form of mental illness.

So what was I to do with the evil spirits I saw, smelled, felt, and heard? Did I imagine these beings? As a child, I wondered if everyone saw the spiritual world but kept quiet about it—maybe they were threatened by their own beasties.

But at the same time, if they did see these tormentors, I hoped some adult could do something about them. They did not. Perhaps they were just my imagination? Still, little ones should not have to wrestle with these thoughts.

As I got older, I learned they were not my imagination. Demons do exist, and they are evil supernatural beings. However, I did not know for many years that their power can be limited by the very creatures they are malevolently driven to destroy—human beings.

Are there different types of demons?

Yes, there are many different types of demons, and I will describe several of them in other stories in this book. But there are only two classifications (my terms). The demons in Class One have power to work solely by becoming joined to people. Class Two demons have no desire to be bound to humans because their responsibility is to influence the spirit world around people. Beastie was a Class One spirit given the right through generational/ancestral sin to attend my way since my birth. (More on generational sin in a bit.)

Why wasn't I surprised by the beast's presence in the hospital?

As I processed this experience through the years, I wondered why a three-year-old wouldn't have reacted more dramatically to a scary creature in their room. Eventually, I realized that the hospital room was not my first introduction to it. Beastie regularly lurked in shadows, crouched in my closet, or hid behind my bedroom door. I had successfully ignored it for so long that I wasn't startled by it anymore. How can this be?

Unless you were very well protected as a child, you were probably exposed to far more trauma than adults usually are. Why? You were physically smaller. You were usually unable to escape from a situation, a possibility you now take for granted. You were surrounded by people who were larger and ranked much higher, so you often experienced defeat or else feared and avoided it. And a great many experiences were new and potentially scary to you.

Further, a child's mind dissociates more in response to traumatic events because the sense of self is just developing. The younger you were when the traumatic event happened, the fewer self-protections and other coping methods you had that adults readily use to keep from feeling traumatized. For example, if someone behaves horribly toward you now, you can probably stop yourself from feeling that you deserve it. But a child treated horribly is likely to feel very defeated, powerless, and at fault, leading to the need to dissociate.[1] I was used to the presence of the menacing beast. Unbeknownst to me, I was being trained to ignore it and pretend it wasn't there. Unfortunately, tolerating the presence of a demon doesn't make it go away.

Why hadn't the beast approached me before?

Do you remember those if-then statements we learned in elementary school? Their purpose was to help establish deductive reasoning. Deductive reasoning means we can draw conclusions based on at least two true statements, often called premises. Because the statements are true, we know our conclusion based on those two statements is also true. I'll use deductive reasoning to explain why the demon didn't have the right to approach me until this hospital experience.

1. Puppies love to eat puppy food; what goes in will come out in the form of feces. Common house flies are attracted to decaying organic filth such as feces. Therefore puppy feces attract flies.

2. Immoral actions (sin) equal feces because they decay your soul.[2] Beelzebub is a name for Satan and means "Lord of the flies."[3] Demons equal flies. Therefore immoral actions attract demons.

This brings us to the morality topic. Historically, societies have asked, "How should we live and why?" One person's slightly bitter definition of morality is, "Morality is a way that unhappy old folks enjoy making young folks unhappy, too." Another person said, "Good and evil are labels of human behavior and do not exist outside the human mind." Webster's definition of morality is probably the most accepted, "Morality is conformity to ideals of right human conduct."[4]

I'm sure we can agree that there are different schools of thought on what morality is or is not. Though I believe the topic of morality is important, I am not going to debate it. The reason is, as far as demons are concerned, it's not based on what we personally or as a society believe is acceptable or unacceptable behavior. The trouble with immorality is the invisible part, the things that happen to us spiritually when we cross that line. And it's just what the kingdom of darkness does not want us to know.

The truth about sin is the most valuable and heavily guarded treasure of the kingdom of darkness. I know. Sin is pretty much a four-letter word nowadays, but maybe it won't seem so offensive if we can define what sin is and what it is not. I apologize in advance if I step on some theological toes, but sin is not:

- An offense against religious law.
- An action that is felt to be highly reprehensible.
- A serious shortcoming.[5]
- An act of offense against God by despising his persons. (What does that even mean?)
- An act of offense by injuring others.
- An evil human act that violates the rational nature of man as well as God's nature.[6]

These definitions condemn and choke the living love right out of a relationship with God! The most important thing we need to know is that there are two kinds of sin: what we're born with and what we live with. Think of it as nature versus nurture—inheritance versus experience. I see those proverbial rolling of the eyes! I know…there's nothing like explaining one complex idea with another, but please stick with me. Briefly, on the nature versus nurture debate regarding personality:

- Nature = genes and hereditary factors that influence who we are, from our physical appearance to our personality characteristics.
- Nurture = environmental variables that impact our identity, including our

early childhood experiences, upbringing, social relationships, and culture.[7]

For the record, I believe we are who we are as a result of *both* nature and nurture. Now, back to the sin side of this comparison. The Bible tells us that all humans are born into the condition of sin—we are physically alive but spiritually dead.[8] What exactly does this mean? Let's start at the beginning. Adam was a direct creation of God, meaning he was not the offspring of other humans. That's why Luke said it this way, "…the son of Enosh, the son of Seth, the son of Adam, the *son of God*."[9] Every time you see the terms *son of God* or *sons of God* in the Bible, it means they are a direct creation of God. We will discuss the sons of God in our Nephilim conversation later in the book. Back to Adam.

The Book of Genesis says that God created Adam in His *own image* and likeness[10] and put His spirit in him.[11] Then God instructed him, "You may freely eat the fruit of every tree in the garden—except the tree of the knowledge of good and evil. The day you eat its fruit, you are sure to die."[12] So, when Adam and Eve exercised their freedom of choice and ate the forbidden fruit, they died. Oh, not physically, but God's spirit left them, resulting in their spiritual death. The story of Adam goes on to say that when he was 130 years old, he had a son in his likeness, *in his image*.[13] From that point on, people were not born from the line of God. We are born from the line of Adam—spiritually dead. This is why Jesus said, "Humans can reproduce only human life, but the Holy Spirit gives birth to spiritual life. So don't be surprised when I say, 'You must be born again.'"[14]

That is the inherited sin nature—the condition of sin. It explains the often quoted scripture, *for all have sinned and fallen short of God's glory*.[15] This verse is not talking about acting immorally; it's talking about being dead spiritually. When Adam disobeyed, sin entered the world. Adam's sin brought spiritual death, so death spread to everyone, for everyone sinned.[16] Yes, Adam's one sin brought condemnation for everyone, but Christ's one act of righteousness brings a right relationship with God and new life for everyone.[17] The remedy for spiritual death is spiritual rebirth. We must be born again to fix our condition. But your body isn't reborn—you don't turn into a newborn baby. And your soul isn't reborn. Your mind doesn't get erased and rebooted. To be born again means only your spirit is birthed, and God's spirit comes to live with your spirit.

The first kind of sin is a spirit issue. But the second kind of sin and the one demons use to bind themselves to us, has to do with our actions—it is a soul issue. We talked about what sin is not. So here's a simple definition of what sin is: it's a willful act of rebellion against the known laws of God. Meaning I know God's Word says not to get drunk, but I do it anyway. Before you toss this book into the trash, please hear me out. I am *the last* person to judge you for your choices. If you continue to read the rest of this, you'll see I was definitely a party girl Friday and Saturday nights and a Sunday morning pew warmer at the same time.

It was life-changing for me when I understood the contrast between the condition of sin and committing sins! Learning that committing a sin would not send me to Hell was beyond a relief. But equally as valuable to me was understanding that each time we sin, we grant the spirit inspiring that action the right to attach to us.[18] This spiritual law is not something I was taught growing up in the faith. If you were also raised in church, I'm willing to bet you didn't see a clever Sunday School felt board lesson illustrating this truth. I know I didn't. In fact, this is a subject most people standing behind a pulpit don't address at all. We can't blame them, however. Because usually, either they are not educated on the topic or have not experienced helping demonized people. They cannot teach what they do not know.

So, what spiritual law gives the kingdom of darkness the legal right to become bound to us? And how does that happen? It begins with temptation. My husband, Timothy, explains this very thoroughly in the Cleansing Seminar.[19]

What is a temptation? Very simply, a temptation is a demon talking. That's all it is. Everybody's heard them. Everybody's been tempted. Sometimes you'll get a thought, and when it comes to your mind, you even feel guilty for having the thought. Has that ever happened to you? I think, oh Lord, how can I be a Christian and think this way? When in reality, it's the enemy. The Bible says the kingdom of darkness can plant thoughts and imaginations in our minds.[20] I don't completely understand how they do that, but I know the Word of God is true. Somehow demons can speak at a pitch that bypasses my outer ear and goes right to the inner ear, somewhat like a dog whistle. The torment is real, and because we don't audibly hear it, sometimes we don't discern what's happening, and they wear us down.

Every Bible illustration of a person being tempted reveals there was a spirit behind that temptation. Matthew 4:1 says, "Then Jesus was led by the Spirit into the wilderness to be tempted there *by the devil.*" There was a spirit behind that temptation. Every Bible illustration of a person who sins reveals there was a spirit talking to them. When Adam and Eve sinned, was there a spirit behind that sin?[21] Sure there was! So our conclusion is this: behind every sin is a spirit.

It's a constant battle that everybody has to wrestle with, which is why Ephesians 4:27 says that when we sin, we give that spirit a place in our life. This is very important. The Greek word for place is *topos*,[22] and it means ground, flesh, and dust. It's referring to our souls. When we sin, we're doing more than simply making a mistake. We're doing more than rebelling against God. The Bible says that when we sin, we give to the spirit that tempted us a place of habitation. That sin becomes the glue that hooks the demon to his place. And the more we continue to commit that same sin, the bigger and bigger the hook becomes. After years of sin, what begins as a small hook becomes a significant place of control.[23]

Where is a demon's "hook" located in me?

Human beings are complex and unique creatures. Speaking strictly physically, the human body is a marvel. Every physical movement we make originates in the brain. It regulates breathing, digestion, and heart rate with no conscious effort. If you live to be 80 years old, your heart will beat approximately 3,363,840,000 times! That's over 3 billion heartbeats![24] It just keeps ticking.

The part of us that makes up our thoughts, feelings, and choices is our soul. The Greek philosopher, Plato, called the three parts of the soul the *logos* (mind or reason), the *thymos* (emotions), and the *eros* (desires or choices).[25] The New Testament often interchanges the words heart and soul, but they generally mean the same thing. The soul is the seat of our thoughts, desires, purposes, understanding, intelligence, character, and will. The 1st Century Romans were well-educated in this concept. So when Paul wrote to them and said, "it is by believing in your *heart* that you are made right with God, and by confessing with your mouth that you are saved,"[26] they understood that their soul was the key to right relationship with God; not how many good acts with which they were credited.

Now, what sets us apart from other living creatures is the immortal human spirit (and opposable thumbs, but we don't need to go into that). Our spirits are the centers of our identity. They are quite independent of social conditioning, personal experience, and character. The soul is the connector between the spirit and the body. It's like it stands with one foot in the spirit and one foot in the body. The spirit and soul live eternally after our bodies are deceased. This simple diagram illustrates these different parts.

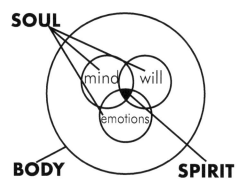

So, where is the demon's hook located in me? The location of this connector is in the same place for the Christian and the non-Christian. This is a very controversial concept in Church circles because most Christians believe they are protected from direct demonic influence. But we all must abide by laws on this planet, whether we are Christians or not. There are physical laws, and there are spiritual laws. For example, let's look at the physical law of gravity. If a Christian and a non-Christian jump off the Empire State building, which one will hit the ground? Of course, they both will. The law of gravity will definitely win.

It's the same thing with spiritual laws. If a Christian and a non-Christian both commit murder, which one will give the spirit of murder a place in their soul? Both of them. But wait a minute, Denise. Are you saying a Christian can be demon-possessed? No, that's not what I'm saying.

The definition of possession is who controls the spirit, not the soul. Because I'm born again, I'm possessed by Jesus Christ. He inhabits the same place as my spirit. That spiritual place can have a powerful demon inside if that person dedicates themselves to Satan and invites his total control. And many people on this planet will not serve any other spirit other than themselves. They aren't hard to spot. You probably know a few of them.

If possession is defined as who controls the spirit, then bondage is who controls the soul—mind, emotions, and will. Now here's where the arguing usually starts. They say, "I thought when I got born again, all this was taken care of. I accepted Jesus Christ as Lord; now I'm a new creation, and all things have passed away. I don't have to worry about that stuff in the past anymore."[27] (That's the overly quoted 2 Corinthians 5:17 free pass verse.)

Remember, just one thing happens when we are born again. Only our spirit is born again. And that spiritual birth makes it possible for the soul to begin to be renewed, restored, healed, and delivered. That's a process that doesn't happen instantly. We are instantly born again, instantly alive in Christ. But the process of cleansing the soul from the demonic hooks, taking back the places in our soul that we gave to that enemy, sometimes takes a matter of years. It did for me. (To discover more on this topic, go to https://www.cleansingthechurch.com/cleansing-seminar.)

Then where is the demon's hook located in us when we sin? I think you know the answer. The spirit doesn't sin. The body doesn't sin. We know that sin is a willful choice to rebel, so the hook must be in the soul where the mind, emotions, and will are located.

I knew nothing about these spiritual laws in that tiny tent bed in the bland pediatric hospital room. I didn't know someone in my previous generations invited Beastie to set up house in our family. Nor did I understand why I was targeted or what to do about it. But now I do.

Alfred Tennyson said, "A lie that is half-truth is the darkest of all lies." I lied when I told my mother it was okay if she went home. But it was far from being okay! I was afraid to be alone with the beast. The lie seemed innocent because it was what some classify as a "white lie." They justify that it shouldn't be wrong since I didn't tell it for an evil reason; I said it to protect my mother. I don't know if it was the first time I ever lied, but it is the first instance I vividly remember because of the dreadful consequences. Before, Beastie simply stalked me. But beginning that moment, the miserable creature was bound to me. And for many years, it persisted in its mission to break down my will to be powerless against it.

CHAPTER FOUR

Facing the Darkness

Speeding down the interstate with the radio blaring, I have only one thing on my mind...*fun!* I never mind the hour-long drive to the small college town, though the scenery is far from exciting. The rolling hills spotted with grazing cattle and golden corn fields are dull surroundings for an eighteen-year-old college student. But, they are only sixty-five short odometer clicks between a sequestered home life and a weekend of mind-numbing thrills.

The excitement I crave is found in extracurricular college life activities. Holly is my closest high school friend and a student at a large Midwest state university. I am a working student enrolled in a boring community college deficient in frat house pajama and toga parties—in fact, no parties whatsoever. Like I said, boring. So as often as my work schedule permits, I make the journey—sometimes for a weekend, many times for only the night.

"So, where's the party?" I inquire with anticipation, bouncing into Holly's dorm room.

"I met a guy in my chemistry class, and he invited us to a party in his room tonight. Nothing big...just three or four of his friends and *US!*" Holly replies, brushing her shoulder-length golden hair back and locking it in place with a cloud of hairspray. We are a striking pair. Holly is tall, thin, and green-eyed; I'm petite, shapely, and golden-eyed. We spell trouble for any young males we set our sights on.

"Great!" I squeal. "What are we waiting for?" And, with that, we skip out the door, down the hallway, into the crisp night air. After a few blocks, the darkness of night gradually grows to a thicker shade of pitch. The moon is absent, but even if it weren't, it would be pretty hidden as the sky is filled with dense clouds. Streetlights and campus lamps provide the only outdoor illumination tonight. Initially, one might attribute the gloom to the cloud cover, but this darkness carries a sinister weightiness. In hindsight, I should not have dismissed it.

Though the campus is bustling with young people hollering, laughing, and chattering, the atmosphere feels as if it's moving in slow motion. It reminds me of that moment when the barometric pressure suddenly drops, and a spawned tornado plunges out of the sky to strike the Earth. It is a mixture of excitement and fear, with a sprinkle of evil wrapped up in the wind. I love it!

Bottomless shadows appear within clusters of young people on street corners and treetops. These shadows do not stir with the wind like the tree shadows or stand still like the building shadows. They leech onto people, slink under cars, and crawl in street gutters. I do my best to ignore them. And I am inexplicably comforted to see Beastie strut alongside us.

I'm beginning to feel anxious until I glance over my shoulder and notice two tall, imposing angels following closely behind us. They are strongly built—one is red-haired with shoulders nearly half as broad as he is tall, the other identical in size but dark and more intimidating. I feel safer knowing they are close on our heels. All the same, I pick up the pace.

As if escorting us to an important appointment, a different creature appears. This spirit is certainly curious. Front ways, it appears to be a beautiful raven-haired woman with exquisite feminine features. From behind, it is an upright, snakelike lizard. I pray it is a coincidence that it slithers before us, but there is a knowing voice in the back of my mind whispering that this is no accident.

We skip to the main entrance of a twelve-story brick dormitory; I freeze. Lowering my voice, I ask Holly if there is another door we can use. She thinks there's one on the other side of the building. I am relieved. "Good! I think that will be faster because the lobby is jammed with people," I quickly reason. Holly seems preoccupied with the fun we are about to experience, and she doesn't give the request a second thought. What she doesn't perceive are the two hulking, half-human, half-dog sentinel demons posted on either side of the building's main entrance. Their leering, canine eyes dart about, surveying individuals who enter or exit through that door. *I do not desire to be observed.* Before the woman/lizard could pass us off to the sentinels, we duck around a corner out of sight.

"Everyone, I would like you to meet Denise, my best friend from high school," Holly announces as we step into chemistry friend Jack's narrow, train-car-sized dorm room. The sum total of room contents is, in order of their appearance, prison-status iron bunk beds, two painted wood dressers, one stained not so gently used lounge chair, and a few stolen university folding chairs.

Apparently, the party had begun several hours earlier that afternoon because the three guys in the room are toasted! They generously pass the marijuana bong to us as if it is simply a can of pop. Lifting a brown grocery bag folded at the top, one of the guys says, "We're only halfway through. Party on!" Over the next few moments, I was informed that the bag was completely full of marijuana a couple of hours ago.

From its lounging spot atop the dresser at the foot of the iron bunk bed, the demon's huge yellow eyes nearly pop out of its head when we enter the room. Instantly its breathing begins to come in rapid shallow hisses as every inch of its being becomes acutely aware that its space was just invaded. Comically, it tries to cover vulnerable body parts by hiding behind a stereo speaker. In a scratchy, high-pitched whisper, I hear it say, "How did *they* get in here without us being informed?"

"Why are you asking me?" another voice fires back from under the bed. "I do not have information on this girl. My host," referring to Jack, "has no spiritual tie to her in any way."

Now a larger, more "in charge" looking demon standing near Jack steps out of the shadows and addresses the other two spirits. "What is your problem, you sniveling imbeciles? Get out of your hiding places before the Commander hears of your cowardice! His probe is just down the hall and will walk through that door any minute now." The sniveling spirits creep out of their dark places and step behind the enormous spirit, using it for protection. This conversation exchange is confusing to me, and I feel pretty uncomfortable, but I do my best to ignore them. Besides, they obviously have a right to be here. The two tall angels who followed us through the streets also followed us into the room. So did the beast. I imagine that's why the demons are agitated.

Two of the three boys live in the party room, and for many moments, they concentrate their full attention on their music collection. They play a partial song from one rock album, then suddenly find another of more interest and switch to that one. After hearing twenty song bites in five minutes, resembling something more like noise hiccups than music, a guttural snicker escapes from the demon next to the speaker. The boys do not recognize its work, but with its long bony finger, it points out album choices for them. Each song invites another half dozen or more assorted demons to enter the room and join the party. Within a short time span, the eight by twelve-foot dorm room contains two girls, two angels, three boys, and upwards of about one hundred and twenty demons. It is *definitely* getting crowded.

"We obviously have this situation under control," boasts the larger spirit as it addresses the small demonic squad. Gesturing toward us, he mockingly laughs and mimics us by dramatically blowing yellow sulfurous smoke rings into the air. "These mortals amuse me. They are easily destroyed simply because they are stupid!"[1] Then flipping us off with its bony finger, we are dismissed,, and the demon returns to its secluded resting place.

Eventually, the boys choose one album to play through. Since I arrived, I have exerted great effort to resist becoming annoyed by their music. Heavy metal is nearly last on my music genre "like" list, and that's the only thing they have played so far. Well, as all good '70s and '80s metal bands will do, this album contains a song entirely backmasked—reverse-recorded. This song captures my attention for no apparent reason, so I lie back and quietly listen. Rather than hearing only twisted staccato tones, I hear clearly pronounced words. As I closely concentrate on what is said, it sounds like it's delivering an alternate message.

"Did you guys hear that?" I blurt. Three pairs of red-glazed eyes stare back at me as if I'd spoken to them in a foreign language. I go on to explain. "They just said, *'You know Satan holds the keys to the lock.'* Listen! Play it again…I want you to hear this." Looking gravely interrupted, they reluctantly restart the song.

"I don't hear what you're saying. You're such a trip, Denise," Holly nervously giggles. "I told you guys you would like her."

Though Holly is accustomed to experiencing interesting and sometimes bizarre situations when we're together, this was a first even for me. Soon I realized that whether or not there is a hidden message in the song is irrelevant because it was simply the catalyst to incite a spiritual reaction.

"Seth will be really entertained by this chick," one roommate says to the other, referring to me.

"For sure! He should be here any minute," chimes in the other roommate.

As if on cue, the much-anticipated Seth ambles into the room. This sets into play an animated commotion of demons jerking and scrambling to their feet at attention. They know precisely who this mortal is! I suppose he is rather renowned in this not-so-spiritually insignificant college town. In fact, Seth is just what the dark kingdom needs in this region to "put them on the map." And that he did. But, to look at him, one would believe he was as ordinary as any other farm boy in the state.

The two angels who accompanied us also take notice of Seth, for the mark of his Satanic purpose is enough to identify him. Though I didn't understand what it was then, spiritually imprinted on his forehead was a circle with a triangle inside it. I now know it was a thaumaturgic triangle used to evoke and summon demons and the spirits of the dead. Judging by his demonic entourage, he had attained more dark spiritual power and position than most Left Hand Path pagans three times his age. Instinctively, the two angelic guards ready themselves for battle. In hindsight, I wish I had taken that opportunity to leave the room. Instead, I choose to tune them out. Beastie was oddly unmoved by all of this and remained on my right side.

I am not impressed with Seth in the least. Maybe it's because he isn't my type or because when he passed me on his way to the other end of the room, he seemed too nonchalantly confident for my taste. No matter, I turn a cold shoulder in his direction and start a conversation with Holly. We try to ignore them, but the boys are animatedly filling Seth in on the earlier back-masking incident. No matter how incredibly they describe the tale, Seth looks bored. He tries to change the subject and becomes downright agitated when they return to it.

Seth grumbles at them to give him some space and pass the bong. And, by the way, why don't these potheads have some alcohol to wash the bad taste out of his mouth? One of the boys quickly leaves the room to get a bottle of something intoxicating, and another gives Seth the water pipe.

Holly and I exchange questioning looks and begin discussing our exit strategy. This Seth is a little too "Lord of the Manner," and since the night is relatively young, we decided it would be much more fun to hit the dance clubs. But now, he's talking about me behind my back though he isn't talking about backmasking. He's talking about my pathetic "guards." I whip around, intending to ask Seth what guards he is referring to, but stop short when I realize he isn't speaking to anyone—not out loud, anyway. His eyes are closed, and he appears to be enjoying the mellowing effects of the pot he's been inhaling. I lean back in my seat in a state of confusion.

"Holly, did you hear Seth talking about me?" I whisper.

"No. He's been sitting there alone since he ordered his royal subjects away from him," she sarcastically replies. It begins to dawn on me that I overheard Seth's spirit talking to…well, I guess any spirit that was listening to him.

What happens next, in reality, occurs in only eight or ten seconds. But any war-seasoned soldier caught in crossfire would describe it as nothing less than a hellishly endless moment. I glance covertly toward a shadow that entered with Seth and half-conceals his face. Something catches my eye.

I didn't know it then, but this moment was a turning point for me. From the hospital room to this dorm room, I had spent my entire life fearfully closing the spiritual eyes with which I could see, hopeful that what dwelt in the darkness would simply go away. But this time, I fix my eyes on the darkness, for within it is a face. A dark, spiritual face. It is stunned when it realizes I can see it! I suppose it has not come across this often—not only a seer but one who doesn't shriek or run away from it. It rustles its flesh-covered wings in a regal, preening fashion and stands taller with an intimidating air of royalty and power. I can hear the faint scratching of its talons on the tile floor as it shifts its weight. These sounds are quite familiar to my own beastie.

For some reason, I don't feel afraid this time—only strangely curious. This unusual calm seems to agitate the beast. As its agitation increases to anger, a low gurgling growl rises from deep within its throat, and foul vapors escape through its nostrils.

Seth's eyes pop open, but he appears to look into another universe. He jolts sideways like he is avoiding an object hurled at him. The longer I sit looking at him, or should I say looking at his creature, the more uncomfortable Seth becomes. The more uncomfortable Seth becomes, the tighter the spirit's needle-sharp fingers grip the young man's neck. Now the other demons in the room grow more intimidating, swiftly moving to position themselves between Seth and me.

Just then, numerous angelic warriors appear seemingly from thin air and storm the room. Like flies scattered by raindrops, the demons begin flying every which way. Some draw swords and stand their ground, while others scramble to escape by any means possible. The angel warriors brandish their weapons, furiously pierce, chop, and thrust them into the now dazed and confused demons. Oh, the stench! With each blow, a putrid odor of rotten eggs mingled with burning garbage fills the room.

This spiritual battle is far more than Seth can withstand. He had attained an incredible amount of power, but no one had prepared him for this kind of warfare. Though he cannot see the battle, the poor soul certainly feels each blow the kingdom of darkness sustains. Seth musters every ounce of strength he can find and channels it to his legs, willing them to stand him on his feet and take him to the door. He crawls out of the shadow in slow motion moving his long, spindly legs with great effort as if leaning into the wind or trudging through waist-high water—his great beast never releasing its grip on Seth's neck. Is he making his way to me? Once Seth is only steps away, his hand shoots up to his face refusing even to look at me.

As Seth crosses my path, his demon receives such an unexpected blow that it is propelled into the bunk bed across from me. Because of his beast's relentless neck grip, pitiable Seth is physically heaved into the heavy iron-framed bunk bed with such force that the whole unit moves two feet closer to the wall on the other side. He lays there half-conscious on his back for several seconds twitching and writhing, eventually wetting himself.

Immediately the demons flee, screeching in terror, the stench of their fumes filling the room. Jack and another guy help Seth to his feet and out the door. On the way out, Jack turns and squares up with me. "What did you do to him?" he accuses.

"I didn't do anything. I was just sitting here minding my own business."

"No, you weren't. I know you did something to Seth. Something like that doesn't happen to someone like him. Get the *h#!!* out of my room! Holly, your friend is a freak. I don't ever want her here again."

Grateful for the opportunity, we escape down the long hallway. "Denise, I know you didn't lay a hand on Seth. But who or *what* did?"

This was a mystery I tried to solve for many, many years.

CHAPTER FIVE

Debriefing the Demonic in the Dorm Room

*The secret of power is the knowledge
that others are more cowardly than you are.*
Ludwig Börne

Demons conduct the entirety of their business based on this secret. They are violent and intimidate with overconfident threats to gain their power. Their methods are successful within their kind and with most humans. However, they are not successful with angels. This is because angels understand their spiritual authority, and demons cannot bully them.

Since angels and demons co-exist in the same spirit world, how does that work? What can they do to each other? What are their rules when it comes to influencing people? The dorm room story illustrates interesting interactions between people, angels, and demons. Let's talk about them.

Why could the angel in this story protect me when the angel in the hospital room could not?

The answer to this question depends on to whom the demon is attached. The demon in the hospital room was a family/ancestral spirit given the legal right by my former generations to try to influence me. It was patiently biding time until I violated an immoral law allowing it to be attached to me. The angel in the hospital room did not have a legal right to interfere with the demon because of the demon's legal right.

The demons in the dorm room were attached to the guys in the room but not to me. The hulking spirit that gripped Seth's neck was powerful, and he acquired the beast through seriously evil satanic ceremonies. When Seth and his ruling spirit passed by, the angel with me gave it a severe warning emphasizing that it did not have a right to attack me.

What gives evil spirits the right to follow us?

Here are a few specific legal rights:

Word Curses

• "Without knowing the force of words, it is impossible to know more."
– Confucius.
• "Words have no power to impress the mind without the exquisite horror of their reality." – Edgar Allan Poe.
• "It doesn't matter if you and everyone else in the room are thinking it. You don't say the words. Words are weapons. They blast bloody holes in the world. And words are bricks. Say something out loud, and it starts turning solid. Say it loud enough, and it becomes a wall you can't get through."
– Richard Kadrey, *Kill the Dead*.
• "Death and life are in the power of the tongue, and those who love it will eat its fruit." – Proverbs 18:21.
• "Your life mainly consists of three things! What you think, what you say, and what you do! So always be very conscious of what you are co-creating!"
– Allan Rufus, *The Master's Sacred Knowledge*.
• "False words are not only evil in themselves, but they infect the soul with evil." – Socrates.

The creative power of words is one of the most important laws that govern the spiritual realm. Words are a powerful force that can create good and evil; how we speak essentially conceives what happens to us and others. Words not only frame how we think but are also spiritual forces. They can be a blessing or a curse. God said He set before us life and death, blessing and cursing; so choose life, that both you and your descendants may live.[1]

One way curses work is when we use our own words to pronounce one upon ourselves. An excellent example of this is what Truman Capote wrote, "Be anything but a coward, a pretender, an emotional crook, a whore: I'd rather have cancer than a dishonest heart." Mr. Capote died twenty-six years later from liver cancer at age fifty-nine. Why? Probably because a demon of cancer was just waiting for Mr. Capote to give it the open door, legal right, to bring sickness to him. I'm sure he didn't intend to curse himself. But demons are keenly legalistic and use our exact words.

Famous sorcerer and occult author Damien Mulkrin outlines four easy steps to put curses on your enemies. He declares, "Sorcerers, witches, and warlocks aren't the only people who can cast spells and put curses on people. With a little training, anyone can do it — even you." Important to note is that steps one and four require whispering words. First: "Evil, live, live, evil." The following two steps involve your thoughts and emotions toward your victim, specifically envisioning the action you desire to happen to them and savoring their agony. Step four, whisper: "Powers of darkness, make this so." Mulkrin says, "If you are sincere in your desire to punish an enemy and have absolutely no reservations about bringing him harm, the curse will work."[2]

But, when it comes to curses, there is another spiritual law at work, and it's this: "As the fluttering bird, as the swooping, diving, twisting swallow; so the curse causeless shall not alight" (Proverbs 26:2). What does this mean? It means if we have done nothing to deserve a curse sent to us, it will not rest upon us. It can literally go back to the one sending it because their motives are evil. Evil equals opened spiritual door.

Family/Ancestral Spirits

The beast in my hospital room was this kind of spirit. Each of us has at least one demon assigned to follow us from the beginning of our days. I know that could sound disturbing, but try not to take it too personally. Demons, or any spirit, have no power unless they can control a human soul. This makes human souls *the* commodity on this planet.

As I've said before, the spirit world is governed by spiritual laws. One of these laws is that once a demon attaches to a soul, it has the legal right to stay in that family for the next four generations. So, if a spirit attached to you someday persuades your great-grandchild to accept it or commit an immoral act, it can pursue four more generations after your great-grandchild. This is a family or ancestral spirit. The spiritual law used here to benefit the demon is found in the Hebrew Bible in several verses, but specifically in Numbers 14:18, "Jehovah is patient and abundantly merciful, forgiving punishment for transgressions (violating a spiritual law); but He by no means clears the guilty, visiting the punishment of the fathers on the children to the third and fourth generations."

Exaggerated Emotions

Anger, unforgiveness, bitterness, fear, sorrow, and hopelessness can be powerful and common emotions. Expressed in moderation, they are pretty harmless. But harbored, brewed, rehearsed, indulged in, and they open the door wide to a demon to attach to your soul. Miguel de Cervantes Saavedra[3] said, "Make yourself honey, and the flies will devour you." Meaning that any emotion you are saturated in can attract an evil spirit to you. Once it has the legal right to be bound to you through expressing excessive emotion, the spirit begins to control you in that area.

Let's look at fear as an example. J.R.R. Tolkien wrote in *The Children of Húrin*, "A man that flies from his fear may find that he has only taken a shortcut to meet it." This is a spiritual law: your fears will come upon you. The Book of Job says in chapter three and verse twenty-five, "For the thing I greatly feared has come upon me." If you are experiencing anxiety, indecision, agitation, or jealousy, then you are afraid of something. You best do some introspective investigation to save yourself a world of hurt.

Laws of Attraction

Let me just come out with it and apologize if you, like me, bristle at general explanations because this explanation is grievously general concerning what it deserves. But for the sake of time and the fact that many would doze off, I'll be brief. Merriam-Webster defines Karma as "the force created by a person's actions that causes good or bad things to happen to that person." Known in other words as, "You get what you give," "What goes around comes around," and "You reap what you sow."[4]

The philosopher/mathematician/scientist Plato postulated in 391 BCE that "likes tend toward likes." Job 4:8 says, "As I have observed, those who plow evil and those who sow trouble reap it." This spiritual law illustrates how we attract a demon with the bait of our actions.

For example, Tom was an onsite apartment superintendent, and the landlord ordered him to demand rent from a delinquent tenant. Now, Tom is a small man with a less-than-average build who spent most of his life trying to prove he was a bigger man on the inside than he was on the outside. Ordinarily, folks were intimidated by his bullishness and steered clear: mission accomplished.

So, armed with self-importance, Tom barged his way to 3B and pounded on the door. When the door opened, Tom commenced wagging his finger in the tenant's face and snarling his demands with an I'm-going-to-show-this-clown-who's-boss attitude. His everyday communication style was direct and antagonistic, but Tom was downright abusive this night. However, it quickly became apparent that he met his match. Mr. 3B was equal in size and shape to Tom but just as furious. After a generous exchange of verbal blows, vile curses, and demeaning names, Tom dismissed Mr. 3B and returned to his apartment.

Ten minutes later, there was a rap at his door. Unaware of his recent dealings with the tenant, Tom's eight-and-a-half-month pregnant wife waddled to the door. There stood Mr. 3B with his loaded double-barrel shotgun aimed directly at her chest. In a blind rage, he unloaded both barrels blasting Tom's wife and unborn child across the room, killing them both.

Tom sowed rage with his words and his actions. Early in his life, he opened the door of his soul to a demon of rage and anger, allowing it to control his behavior. Regrettably, his innocent wife and unborn child reaped the fruit of it.

Witchcraft and Voodoo

No one likes to feel powerless or controlled. The desire for power is the crux of every war and in the heart of each person who has suffered at the hands of a bully. World governments and many religions use their power to control lesser or oppressed individuals. Just as guns can be used for good purposes (self-defense, obtaining food, sport), they can also be used for evil purposes (murder, suicide, accidents). People who perform witchcraft and voodoo use these practices for good and evil purposes. Whichever their goal, power and control are necessary to accomplish it.

Witches (sometimes called Wiccans) believe that the magic of witchcraft is the result of imposing their will upon the world by projecting it through mystical channels, such as invoking the power of spirits through a spell. The witch endeavors to draw in enough "outside" power for the spell to be effective. They use the power of a demon, but due to ignorance of the spiritual world, many do not believe this is so. They believe that if they develop a strong ethical core and commitment to perform rituals correctly, they can control what happens to themselves and others. They use tools such as candles, geometric shapes, plants, herbs, soil, water, fire, chalices, and bells, to name a few. A demon can attach to any of these items the witch chooses because that is the only thing the demon needs of the witch—their will.

Voodoo is similar to witchcraft because it utilizes rituals and tools to accomplish goals. In contrast to witches, a Voodoo practitioner does not believe they are a powerful person who orders spirits to do their bidding. They see themselves as servants of the spirits, presenting them with offerings and even animal sacrifices to solicit their power. Like witches, they use tools to accomplish their good or evil tasks. One tool most of us are familiar with is a Voodoo doll. The doll can be used for love, power, domination, luck, and harm.

Here's the method used to make a Voodoo doll:

Step 1

Using a Voodoo straight pin, they label the doll by pinning to it either a picture or the name of the targeted person. This next step gives the demon the right to follow and influence the targeted person. (Remember how once upon a time I began answering the question, *What gives evil spirits the right to follow us?* Well, here's the answer.)

Step 2

Make the doll "become" the person by attaching or inserting something familiar to that person. These items can be a lock of hair, a nail clipping, a piece of their clothing, or anything they own. Voodoo dolls work because even though the targeted person no longer possesses their personal items, they are still connected to them through a spiritual ownership tie. This tie is invisible to most people unless you see the spiritual world.

After a long training period, voodoo priests and priestesses perform rituals that open themselves to spiritual possession. Again, due to ignorance of the spirit world, they believe that if they invite only good spirits in, then that's what they'll get. A demon will act "good" for as long as it takes to get a human to choose to open the door of their soul to it. And when the person shows any sign of opposing the demon, it'll turn on them with a legal right to abuse them.

What are warrior angels?

A warrior angel was responsible for the blow against Seth's demon resulting in its collision with the iron bunk bed. It was probably confusion and near panic that motivated it to come in such close proximity to the angel.

Warrior angels are precisely as their name sounds: angels that fight spiritual battles with evil forces. I think they are the most interesting of all the angels to observe. But sadly, like archangels, they have been vastly mythologized by writers and artists for centuries. If you do a Web search on "warrior angels," you'll view thousands of artists' ideas of these powerful beings; however, they are contrived feathery imaginations, some wearing bustiers.

Because I have been involved in hundreds of spiritual cleansings, I have had the opportunity to see many warrior angels. Their job during these battles with evil spirits is to aid the person being cleansed and to escort the spirits from the premises. What I find fascinating about warrior angels is that they always appear to be wearing some sort of uniform. However, on closer inspection, they are not "wearing" the uniform; they *are* the uniform. For example, if they are wearing a helmet, in reality, it is their head shaped like a helmet. If they appear to wear a breastplate, it's their chest formed like a breastplate. Whereas we put on and take off garments, hats, shoes, etc., warrior angels cannot remove these items as they are part of them.

Several years ago, a group of us were traveling to a dangerous region of Africa. One warrior angel traveling with us was entirely bronze in color and appeared to wear a helmet formed with a sharp point in front. His boots/feet duplicated the helmet's sharp point. His arms and hands were swords.

On another occasion, a troop (for lack of a better word) of warrior angels appeared to be wearing capes made up of hundreds of swords. Their legs were sturdier and thicker than human legs. They carried something like fireballs attached to their hands with chains. They looked to be on a reconnaissance mission around the camp's perimeter where we stayed.

Interestingly, none of the warrior angels I've seen look female. They are always fully "clothed." They never have wings.

What types of demons were encountered in this story?

I will sort the demons mentioned in the story into these two classifications: Class One gains power by becoming joined to people. Class Two never binds themselves to humans because their responsibility is to influence the spirit world around people. The first demons we encounter in this story are "bottomless shadows" leeching on people, slinking under cars, and crawling in street gutters. In my opinion, these things are downright creepy! They are malevolent spirits that carry out the bidding of demonic entities in authority above them. Have you ever walked down a dark alley or parking lot and goosebumps prickle your arms, indicating something otherworldly is with you? Or have you ever felt energized by the wind? Often these sensations are the work of this type of demon, which places them in Class Two—never binds themselves to humans because their responsibility is to influence the spirit world around people. Sometimes these shadow spirits dramatically affect a person's mood. For example, if the place where the shadow spirit is bound was once a brothel, a person might suddenly feel overly sexy and desirable under the spirit's influence. If the location where the shadow spirit is bound was once a mental hospital, a person might feel confused and mentally unstable when in that building. But, once they are away from the shadow spirit, their mood returns to normal.

The next spirit we encounter in the story is "a beautiful raven-haired woman" that, from behind, appears as "a hideous reptilian creature—an upright snakelike lizard." This spirit is a Nephilim and doesn't fit into *either* demonic classification. Since it's not fully demonic, for now, I'm not going to expound on this spirit. We will talk about Nephilim a bit later in the book. I promise.

Next, we meet the "two hulking half-human, half-dog sentinel demons posted on either side of the entrance" to the dormitory. These are also Class Two demons. They are demonic guards used to monitor activity and then report to a demon ranking in authority over them. The lower half of their body is furry and looks like a dog, complete with hind legs and tail. But, from the torso upwards, they appear somewhat human, meaning they have two arms, a half-human-half-canine face, and humanlike skin. Some Satanists call these demons sentinels.

Fast forward to the demons already in the dorm room once we arrive. These demons belong in Class One because they have power solely by becoming joined to a person. In this case, they were attached to either Jack or his roommate.

This brings us to the back-masking incident. Just so you don't get the impression that I am morally opposed to Rock music specifically (which I am *not*), let me talk about the part of the story where "each song invites another half dozen or more assorted demons to enter the room and join in the party."

With some help from the lyrics of the nu metal band KoRn's song, *"Twisted Transistor,"* I will explain how demons can use music.

A lonely life, where no one understands you

But don't give up, because the music do, music do

Because the music do

And then it's reaching inside you forever preaching

F#@k you too

Your scream's a whisper

Hang on you

Twisted Transistor

An electrical transistor is a semiconductor that amplifies, controls, and switches signals. Like a light switch on the wall, the transistor acts as a simple on/off switch, preventing or allowing current to flow through it. KoRn's message is that people are music transistors. They have it a bit off the mark by stating that music understands you as if it is a living, discerning entity. The music itself is not a spirit; however, all genres of music are empowered by some type of spirit. A human spirit, the Holy Spirit, or a hellish spirit can inspire music. Therefore, people become transistors of the *spirit inspiring* the music. Think of it like this: the spirit is the electrical current, and the person listening is the on/off switch allowing or disallowing the spirit to flow through them. The dorm room filled with demons "after listening to twenty song bites in five minutes" because the demonically inspired songs used the three boys as their transistors, allowing the demons to flow through them. If any of these guys decided to "embrace" the music, the demon empowering it would be bound to them.

The "demonic entourage" accompanying Seth was bound to his soul. That would put these demons in Class One. Seth was not your average college student. Though he was only nineteen or twenty years old, he was pretty advanced in Satanism—more specifically, what is known today as Theistic Satanism. Theistic Satanism is the worship of Satan as a deity through rituals, sacrifices, and blood covenants. This path taught Seth to pursue great power through ceremonies inviting demons to rule through him. He had gone so far in his pursuit that he had already acquired a satanic purpose. I wonder where he is today, for his future was indeed dark.

If anyone was to be commiserated with in this experience, it was Seth. Though he thought he was the supreme power in this college town, the poor guy didn't even know what hit him. Neither did I—but I do now.

PART 2

Unclean Spirits

CHAPTER SIX

My Soul To Keep

Imagine a perfect April afternoon, the kind that makes you feel carefree and eternal. Fluffy white clouds move southward and occasionally cross the sun, creating island shadows floating over the ground. It is summer-prophesying weather, and the gentle breeze is the prophet.

A handful of classmates and I step through the school's double doors as we set off toward home. It is a good day for walking and taking your time at it. When we are twelve years old, walking home with our peers creates a false sense of maturity and independence, though it only lasts for the thirty minutes of distance it takes to arrive at our back doorsteps. For me, it is well worth the trouble I will get when I come home fifteen minutes late because I "missed" the bus.

The first time I missed the bus was an honest mistake. It was the autumn of 1971 when my second-grade teacher bestowed upon me a hallowed honor—*chalkboard eraser cleaning*. Since the first grade, I have coveted this aggressive act of banging the erasers together. The powdery billow of chalk dust produced was one attractive feature; another was that you could enjoy making this fine mess without adult supervision. This special job took place after school, though, at the time, I didn't understand that the bus wouldn't wait for me to clean the erasers. Poor Miss Sanderson didn't know that I rode the bus home, mostly because I omitted that bit of information when she asked for eraser-cleaning volunteers. Therein lies the conundrum.

So, the bus left the curb at 3:10, and I finished my erasers at 3:15. When I exited the school's front doors to a vacant Fifth Street, a tinge of panic gripped me, and I sat down on the steps to consider my options. I could go to the principal's office and use the phone to call my mother—*boring*—or I could walk three blocks to Grandma and Grandpa's house. The latter won due to the lure of sheer adventure.

This maiden voyage places near the top of my all-time favorite memories list, for it holds a collection of other favorite things. Let's begin with a crisp sunny day that made me grateful for the tights and wool jacket my mother insisted I wear that morning. Also, it just so happened that Mrs. Olson, who lived directly across from the school, was burning leaves in her ditch…a premium favorite. While strolling down Third Avenue, I passed three more burn piles before reaching the block's end. The spicy muskiness of the smoke burned my nose and soaked into my hair. Though it makes me wheeze, the scent of burning leaves still feels like home to me.

Crossing Sixth Street brought me to the fire station where I'd spent many carefree Saturday afternoons climbing on the fire trucks (favorite thing) with my cousins, Doug and Allen. Our fathers served on this volunteer fire department since they were sixteen. Peering through the windows, I discovered the building was vacant and locked up tight. I moved on.

When at the end of the block, I turned right and crossed the street to Mr. and Mrs. Williams' side lot. In springtime, the lilac tree garnishing the corner of the yard is chock full of fragrant periwinkle blooms. However, the star attraction of autumn is the engorged apple tree. Of course, I picked a couple of ripe apples, one to share with Grandpa and one to snack on for the rest of the stroll.

I reached my destination just a half-block past the Williams', then across the railroad tracks. Thankfully, Grandma and Grandpa were home! Delicious toasted wheat bread slathered with real butter, ranking high on my favorite things list, was my reward. After a few minutes of relishing my one-on-one time with Grandpa, he persuaded me to call my mother to tell her I was safely at their home. Needless to say, when Mom arrived, I was chastised, and my "warm fuzzies" came to a screeching halt.

That was the beginning of my bus-missing career. Now that I am twelve, rather than walking merely three blocks to my grand-parents' house, I have broadened my horizons to walk just under one mile to my own house.

The best part of this walk is that it provides the opportunity to meander through the cemetery at the top of our hill, between where the Village of Hampton ends and the fields and forests begin.

The reposeful cemetery is a homey, pretty little thing. It displays an assortment of oak and maple trees planted by God a hundred-plus years ago, ankle-deep grass spattered with aged gray and white tombstones, and is fashionably silhouetted by dense woods trimmed at the edge by wildflowers. If you were to ask, I would be compelled to say I feel this is one of the most peaceful places I have ever frequented. It is my most loved hideaway, my sanctuary. However, to call it a hideaway is not entirely accurate since I am never there alone.

My schoolmates walk along the outermost edge of the grounds closest to the road. This is where we part ways, and they amble home. I take my time wandering up and down the pebbled pathways drawing me into the heart of the cemetery. It has been here since the early 1800s, so I feel it deserves the honor and respect due to an older person. After all, it is a garden sown with people belonging to someone who loved them. There is no fear in this place—only love and sadness.

The boy is here again, as I expected he would be. I see him most visits—you might say he's a regular in this place. He seems a bit young, seven or eight, to visit a cemetery alone, but who am I to judge? Maybe he visits a parent or grandparent. There are usually a half dozen others here walking, weeping, talking to their loved ones. Today, though, there is only the boy. He sits atop the usual tombstone with his eyes focused on the ground as I always find him. His dark hair is thick and wavy. He's a bit pale and a fragile wisp of a little man with a frail frame. I never speak to the folks visiting the cemetery. It seems irreverent to talk to strangers here, as I do not wish to intrude on their private moments. I have said Hello to the boy during other visits, but he only nods in my direction. I feel sorry for him because he appears so deserted. Today I determined I will say more than simply Hello.

"Aren't we having a nice day?" I smile optimistically.

He offers a solitary nod. I forge on. "The warm breeze is waking up the butterflies."

Still, dead silence. "My name is Denise. What's yours?"

Staring at his toes, he whispers, "Adam."

"Adam. That's a nice name. I see you here often."

"Yes, I know."

"You've seen me before?"

"Yes. Every time," he affirms, lifting his unreflecting eyes to mine.

I ask him why he's sad. He says it's because he misses his mother so much. I sit in the cool grass listening as he describes how pretty she was, her blue eyes and wavy hair, and how she sang softly to him when she tucked him in bed at night. He wonders if she went away because he broke the teacup. He explained that one day, he felt weaker than usual. He hadn't been able to eat, and even most liquid wouldn't stay down. To help soothe his tummy, Mama served him warm sweet tea in her favorite cup. He took a sip, and it sure tasted good! Mama made the best tea. But it came right back up, and when he vomited, he dropped the teacup. He tried to fix it, but it wouldn't hold tea anymore. She left soon after that. I try to comfort him, but really, what can soothe his lonely little heart? It's obvious his mother was his world.

The cloud island shadows now stretch out slantways, indicating that I have spent more time talking with Adam than I realized. I tell him I had best get home, thank him for talking to me, and I hope to see him again soon. He says I probably will. Smiling at him and feeling tremendously pleased that I have made a new friend on this perfect afternoon, I turn toward home. After three steps, I remember to ask Adam where he lives.

"Adam, where do you…." But he's gone. I don't mean he is running through the cemetery away from me. No. He is *gone*, as in *vanished*!

Now I notice something I have never seen before—the front of the tombstone where Adam sits. It occurs to me that I have never really looked at it because Adam always sits on top with his legs dangling down, covering the front. The tombstone reads,

"Now I lay me down to sleep,
I pray the Lord my soul to keep."

Beloved Son

Adam Jonathan White

Born May 2, 1921 – Died September 10, 1928

In the center of these loving words is an oval-shaped black and white photo of a dark-haired fragile wisp of a little man with a frail frame.

I visited Adam in this special place from time to time. His physical life on this planet ended far too early, and his spirit was trapped here by his great sorrow and fear of letting his mother go. I do not believe our friendship made him feel less lonely. His heart belonged to his mother as she was his treasure[1]—he was eternally separated from her.

Thomas A. Kempis wrote, "Love feels no burden, thinks nothing of its trouble, attempts what is above its strength, pleads no excuse for impossibility, for it thinks all things are lawful for itself and all things are possible." Sometimes the line between love and obsession is blurred. In Adam's case, this was true.

* * *

What is our fascination with ghosts? Many cultures believe in the afterlife, and though theories vary on how it is experienced, the common thread is that we are simply passing through this physical chapter of life into the spirit world of life after life.

Over the past two decades, the media industry has increased the production of films and television series about displaced spirits unable to "cross over to the other side." A 2016 Harris Poll[2] showed that 64 percent of those surveyed believe in the survival of the human soul/spirit after death, and 42 percent actually believe in ghosts. Is it possible that this interest is driven by a sincere hope that our existence does not end in physical death, that we are immortal, and that there is life after death? Most folks have lost a loved one they desire to see at least one more time to say something they wished they had spoken while living. Maybe they want to embrace them or merely hear their voice again. I have lost such a loved one.

We discussed two kinds of spirits that inhabit the spirit world: good spirits, known as angels, and evil spirits, known as demons. If you also see what I see, you've noticed another kind of spirit commonly called ghosts. I want to refer to them as human spirits because when most people think of ghosts, words like "haunted" and "scary" come to mind. As you can see by reading Adam's story, the human spirits of the deceased are not always scary. They can be very sad and lonely.

So, what is the truth about human spirits? One truth is that their existence proves there *is* life after death. But there's more!

CHAPTER SEVEN

Ties That Bind

Letting go is hard
but being free is beautiful.
Jasinda Wilder

When it comes to the story of Adam, I find it interesting that I catch the most grief over it from no other group other than Christians. It is not the whole gang, but a portion that has labeled me with interesting titles such as necromancer, medium, or witch. These titles are mentioned in the Bible and strictly forbidden as a practice, so I see their perspective. However, it is human nature to fear what we don't understand, and many Christians are afraid of the spirit world more than anything else.

How many of the Ten Commandments[1] can you name? A 2007 survey by Kelton Research found that Americans recalled the seven ingredients of a McDonald's Big Mac more easily than the Bible's Ten Commandments. As a matter of fact, 80 percent of 1,000 respondents could name the burger's primary ingredient—two all-beef patties—but less than 6 in 10 knew the commandment "thou shalt not kill." Just 45 percent of participants could recall the "honor thy father and mother" commandment, but 62 percent knew the Big Mac has pickles.[2]

Okay. Thank you for that random information, Denise. Not only do the Ten Commandments sound old-fashioned, but I can almost hear shackles dragging on the concrete floor just thinking about them! This is how I felt about these tenets for the first half of my life. Except for my respect for them since they are included in the Bible, I viewed them as harsh rules handed down from a stern God ready to lower the hammer on my head if I broke one of those things. Happily, I am living proof that does not happen, as I have broken at least five of them, and not one time did I get bopped.

In my search to understand spiritual laws, I have realized the Ten Commandments are a love letter, a tender, earnest message from the heart of God. I am convinced they are one of the most powerful expressions of God's love in all of Scripture. Why? These ten statements touch virtually every part of our lives. They are loving parameters for humans to live within, providing truth, blessing, strength, and hope for a successful future. But not only that, they are legal boundaries that every entity in the kingdom of darkness is constrained to function within. Without these spiritual laws, their atmosphere cannot move, control, or succeed. So, in some ways, we could say the Ten Commandments are a blessing or a curse. A blessing to us if we live by them so our heavenly Father can fulfill his promises to us. Or a curse to us if we break them and give an evil spirit the legal right to attach to us. Just in case you haven't memorized the Ten Commandments, here's a quick refresher:

1. Have no other gods – Make God first in your life.
2. Do not have idols – Keep the objects of your focus in balance.
3. Don't disrespect God's name – There's power in the name of Jesus.[3] Wield it well!
4. Remember the sabbath – Make time for rest and reflection.
5. Honor your parents – Respect their position in your life and be quick to forgive.
6. Do not murder – Be careful with anger, including heart attitudes towards other humans.
7. Do not commit adultery – Keep your marriage promises.
8. Do not steal – Repay what you borrow.
9. Do not tell lies about others – Words have no wings but they can fly a

thousand miles.

10. Do not be jealous – Happiness comes from contentment.

Since I became acquainted with Adam in the cemetery so many years ago, I have learned quite a bit about unclean spirits. Let's look at the spiritual laws by which humans—dead or alive—are governed. I was surprised to discover those laws are the Ten Commandments.

These are some questions I asked on my journey.

What exactly is a human spirit?

There is an accepted belief in Christian circles that ghosts are demons transforming themselves to look like people. So let me say it plainly: human spirits are *not* demons. The Bible says the people Jesus encountered were not overly impressed that he could cast out demons. This is because they had exorcists who were also doing it. But they were *amazed* unclean spirits obeyed him.[4] Why? Isn't an unclean spirit simply a lewd or filthy demon? No, an unclean spirit is a human spirit whose body has died and is now inhabiting a living person's body. They were a common problem in Jesus' day! So common that you'll find the phrases unclean spirit or unclean spirits twenty-three times in the New Testament.

In Old Testament Hebrew, the word *spirit* is *ruwach* and means "breath" or "breath of life." In New Testament Greek, the word *spirit* is *pneuma* and means spirit. The type of pneuma is identified by the word that comes before it: *Holy* Pneuma, *human* pneuma. An unclean spirit is the breath of life that has departed from a deceased human body. If you're not convinced and need more biblical backup for this concept, I'll direct you to my husband's book, *Unclean Spirits: One of Satan's Best-Kept Secrets*.[5]

Whatever personality traits a human being harbored in life, they will likely retain in death. Because they are dead does not mean they are spooky, creepy, or frightening. Just as some people you know are sweet and gentle, or some are not-so-nice, human spirits are the same. Some are timid spirits, and some violent and pushy ones who will do as they please. They are the person they were when they lived in their bodies.

What do human spirits look like?

Human spirits look like they did at the time of their physical death. I do *not* mean that if they were stabbed to death, they walk around with a knife jabbed in them. Sometimes they do, but most often, they do not. I mean that if they were eight years old upon their death, they appear to be eight years old as a human spirit. Human spirits are not solid like a physical body that occupies space. They are somewhat transparent, but occasionally it takes me a few seconds to determine if I'm seeing a physical person or a spirit. They wear clothing common in the era of their lifetime. Their features are as distinct as they were when they lived—the same hair color, height, body shape, and weight. The only difference is that they do not have a physical body.

To illustrate just how *alive* a human spirit can appear, let's travel 2,000 years back to the Greco-Roman city of Caesarea Philippi in northern Israel, where Jesus brought His disciples the winter before His death. This popular city was located about 30 miles north of the Sea of Galilee on a terrace of Mount Hermon's southern slope. A piece of information that will be more interesting later in this story is that Mount Hermon is the highest mountain east of the Mediterranean Sea and represents the northwestern limit of the Israelite conquest under Moses and Joshua.

But what put first-century Caesarea Philippi on the map were the pagan sanctuaries at the foot of Mount Hermon built by the Greeks to worship the god Pan—worship which included strange sexual acts with goats. The Greeks called this place Panias, and the Cave of Pan was the main attraction. The beautiful Temple of Augustus was built directly in front of it, and the far end of the temple, which normally housed an image of the deity, was open to the mouth of the cave. This orifice allowed Pan's animal sacrifices to be thrown directly into the chasm of the grotto. How convenient for them!

The Cave of Pan, also known in those days as the Gate of Hades (Hades is Greek for Underworld), was amazing for many reasons. The area was lush, and the waters, today called the Banias River, flowed out of the cave and fed the Jordan River. A bottomless pool inside the cave contained so much water that it could not be measured. If animal sacrifices thrown into the pool sank, then Pan was appeased. In this place, the Greeks and Romans received revelations from Pan, who was believed to be a seer and a giver of revelations.[6] This area was so wicked that rabbis forbade a good Jew to come here. With all that in mind, it seems like a peculiar place for Jesus to bring his closest friends. But Jesus did a lot of peculiar things.

Imagine you are one of the disciples standing with Jesus on the Banias River banks in this lovely yet creepy setting. A rocky face rises 100 feet above you and 500 feet wide, centered by the exquisite white marble Temple of Augustus and the foreboding Cave of Pan—the Gate of Hades. Still, Jesus brought you and his brothers here. Why this spot? Because Jesus doesn't choose locations of convenience to make important announcements. He chooses locations of spiritual strategy.

Jesus asks you and his disciples, "Whom do people say that the Son of Man is?"

"Well," they reply, "some say John the Baptist, some say Elijah, and others say Jeremiah or one of the other prophets." For it was prophesied that the Messiah would be preceded by Elijah the prophet.[7]

Then he asks, "But who do you say I am?"

Simon answers, "You are the Messiah, the Son of the living God."

Jesus replies, "You are blessed, Simon, son of John, because my Father in Heaven has revealed this to you. You did not learn this from any human being. Now I say to you that you are Peter (Peter means rock), and upon this rock, I will build my church, and the Gate of Hades shall not prevail against it," as he gestures over his shoulder toward Pan's Cave. "And I will give you the keys of the kingdom of Heaven, and whatever you bind on Earth will be bound in

Heaven, and whatever you loose on Earth will be loosed in Heaven." Then he sternly warns the disciples not to tell anyone that he is the Messiah.[8]

Wow! Jesus drops this in your lap and then orders you not to tell anyone that you are best friends with the Messiah? Why not? Why here? Because it was a powerful way to let the world, both seen and unseen, know that there would be a coming battle for the souls of men. At the foot of this debauched mountain, the gauntlet was thrown at Satan's feet; his time was just about over.

We don't know if they camped out at the cave (doubtful) or stayed in Caesarea Philippi after Jesus declared war on the kingdom of darkness because the narrative picks up a week later. So, on with the story and why I'm using this illustration to support my statement that human spirits appear as living people.

About eight days later, Jesus took Peter (previously known as Simon), John, and James up on Mount Hermon to pray. And as he was praying, the appearance of his face was transformed, and his clothes became dazzling white. Suddenly, two men, Moses and Elijah, began talking with Jesus. They were glorious to see. And they spoke about his departure from this world, which was about to be fulfilled in Jerusalem.[9]

Now, let's just sit with this for a minute. So that we're all on the same page, I'd like to point out that Moses died 1,200 years before this event, and Elijah was taken up to Heaven over 800 years before!

With that in mind, I have a few questions about this story. I imagine you do, too.

Q: Were these two famous Old Testament men actually present, or did the trio have a dream or vision of them?

A: This text from Luke (also repeated in Matthew and Mark[10]) doesn't say that the disciples had a vision or dream of Moses and Elijah. The Bible says Moses and Elijah appeared and conversed with Jesus. Peter, John, and James physically saw and audibly heard these celebrities. A party of four instantly became a party of six!

Q: How did Peter, and presumably the other two, recognize Moses and

Elijah if they had never seen them before? There are at least two possible answers to this question.

A: First, I mentioned that all three gospels place Simon Peter's revelation of Jesus as "the Messiah, the Son of the living God" eight days before this transfiguration. The key to this revelation is that the identity of Jesus is *revealed by the Father*—not put together by the intellect of Peter. The identity of Moses and Elijah at the transfiguration of Jesus was probably revealed in the same way as the identity of Jesus was—through the revelation of the Father.

Second, the identity of the two men talking with Jesus could have been discovered because of their conversation topic—the departure of Jesus. The term "departure" that Luke used is the Greek word *exodos*. Moses, who led the people of Israel in an exodus from Egypt, and Elijah, whose exodus from life was in a fiery chariot ride, probably talked with Jesus about His coming exodus through His death on a cross and resurrection from the dead. This is how Peter most likely recognized that it was Moses and Elijah talking with Jesus.

Q: If Moses died, but Elijah didn't, where did their spirits come from?

A: The answer to this mystery lies in the Underworld.

CHAPTER EIGHT

The Underworld

The road to Hades is the easiest to travel.
Diogenes Laërtius

There is a generous amount of fiction readily available about the Underworld. From Greek mythology to books, movies, music, and video games—someone has something to say about it. The problem is that most of these ideas are dark conjectures and entertaining fantasies. As stated before, I have learned to search the Bible for truth on such subjects and leave make-believe tales to human imaginations.

My truth search about the Underworld began in the Old Testament, which is also where the confusion starts. The Hebrew word for Underworld is *Sheol*. That seems simple. However, Sheol is translated into three different English words: the *grave*, *Hell*, and the *pit*. The Greek New Testament counterpart of Sheol is *Hades*. Hades is not Hell. It is not the Lake of Fire.[1] Instead, Hades and Sheol mean the same thing—the Underworld or the *abode of the dead*.

What are the contents of the Underworld? In the diagram below (after all, I am a visual), we see a place called *Tartarus*. Peter explains the inhabitants of Tartarus this way: "For God did not spare the angels who sinned by leaving their proper domain, but cast them down to Hell (Tartarus) and delivered them into chains of darkness, to be reserved for judgment."[2] Tartarus is not a place of judgment for wicked humans, so Hell is a poor English translation. Jude also speaks about this place for sinning angels. He calls it *a place of ever-*

lasting chains.³ Later in this book, we will discuss these sinful angels who left their proper domain in more detail. For now, we can establish that they are trapped in their own little corner of the Underworld. Though it isn't necessary to delineate these here, the Bible tells us the Lake of Fire and the Bottomless Pit/Abyss are also in the Underworld. The giant chasm running down the middle is about to be explained.

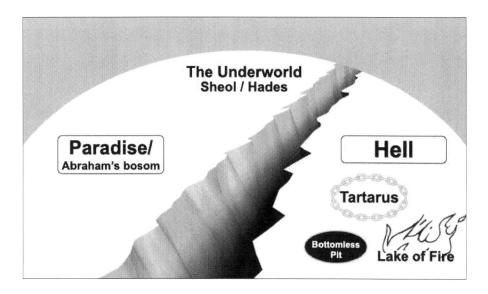

And now, back to my question regarding where Moses's and Elijah's spirits came from when they joined Jesus on Mount Hermon. Next, let's look at a story traditionally known as "The Rich Man and Lazarus." Many people think of this as a parable, as Jesus often used short anecdotes to teach moral lessons. However, I would like to point out that Jesus does not present this story as a parable, and the main point of it is not a moral lesson. Also, in no other parable does Jesus name any of the individuals. We have every reason to believe that Jesus is giving us an actual case history account that He would know. After all, He is the man from Heaven. To help make this clearer, I've added the original Greek words and meanings in parentheses. Jesus tells it like this:

"There was a rich man who dressed in purple and fine linen and who feasted sumptuously every day. But at his gate lay a poor man named Lazarus, whose body was covered with sores, who longed to eat what fell from the rich man's table. In addition, the dogs came and licked his sores. Now the poor man died and was carried by the angels to Abraham's bosom (Paradise in the Underworld). The rich man also died and was buried. And in hell (*hadēs*=the entire Underworld), as he was in torment (*basanos*=Hell), he looked up and saw Abraham far off with Lazarus at his side.

"So he called out, 'Father Abraham, have mercy on me, and send Lazarus to dip the tip of his finger in water and cool my tongue because I am in anguish in this fire.' But Abraham said, 'Child, remember that in your lifetime you received your good things and Lazarus likewise bad things, but now he is comforted here, and you are in anguish. Besides all this, a great chasm has been fixed between us so that those who want to cross over from here to you cannot do so, and no one can cross from there to us.'

"So the rich man said, 'Then I beg you, father, send Lazarus to my father's house. For I have five brothers, and I want him to warn them so that they don't come into this place of torment.' But Abraham said, 'They have Moses and the prophets; they must respond to them.' Then the rich man said, 'No, father Abraham, but if someone from the dead goes to them, they will repent.' He replied to him, 'If they do not respond to Moses and the prophets, they will not be convinced even if someone rises from the dead.'"[4]

These are the important details of this story that will point us in the direction of where Moses's spirit came from when he met Jesus on Mount Hermon:

1. Jesus tells us there is a place in the Underworld where the righteous go upon their death called *Abraham's Bosom*, which is a place of comfort. We know this place is also called *Paradise* because when Jesus was suffering on the cross with two thieves hanging on each side of him, one of them said, "Jesus, remember me when you come into your Kingdom." And Jesus replied, "I assure you, today you will be with me in Paradise."[5] When Jesus died that day, he went to the heart of the Earth and remained there for three days.[6] So in Jesus's day, this place called Abraham's Bosom was also known as Paradise.

2. Jesus teaches us that in the Underworld, there is another region called *Hell*. Again, Hell is not Hades—Hades is the *entire* Underworld. In the Old Testament, Hell is called *Gehenna*. It is a place of torment, a place of endless fire.[7]

3. This story also tells us that there is a giant chasm in the Underworld between Paradise and Hell. That's the great divide in the Underworld diagram (page 71). We know this chasm cannot be crossed because Abraham said to Lazarus, "there is a great chasm separating us. No one can cross over to you from here, and no one can cross over to us from there." Jesus also explains that they could see across this vast chasm. The rich man is in Hell and sees that Lazarus is in a place of comfort. They were close enough to speak to one another across this gulf. How tormenting would this be? Close enough to see and hear each other but unable to cross it.

Now we have half the answer to our earlier question, "If Moses died, but Elijah didn't, where did their spirits come from?" We know that Moses resided in Abraham's Bosom/Paradise after his death because he was a righteous man. So, he came up from Paradise to meet with Jesus on Mount Hermon.

What about Elijah? The author of 2 Kings 2:11, wrote, "As Elijah and Elisha were walking along and talking, suddenly a chariot of fire appeared, drawn by horses of fire. It drove between the two men, separating them, and Elijah was carried by a whirlwind into Heaven."[8] We are told only that Elijah was removed from Earth. The writer says Elijah was taken "to Heaven," but the Hebrew word for Heaven is *shamayim*, which has only three possible meanings: the sky, outer space, or God's throne room. The writer described Elijah's departure from his companion's perspective on the ground, so he could only say that Elijah was taken into the *shamayim*, the sky. Elijah's removal from the ground tells us nothing about what happened to him afterward. We can only know that he did not experience death.[9]

However, we cannot presume that Elijah entered God's throne room in Heaven. Why not? Because Jesus said, "No one has ascended to Heaven but

He who descended from Heaven: *the Son of Man.*"[10] After learning about the story of the Rich Man and Lazarus, we know Elijah's spirit was not floating around outer space nor was he in Heaven. He was transferred to Abraham's Bosom to await the arrival of the Messiah, just like all Old Testament righteous people. God granted him a remarkable departure from the Earth, but He couldn't allow him to enter Heaven before Jesus's death and resurrection.

Now we know that Elijah and Moses resided in Abraham's Bosom when Jesus told his friends the story about the Rich Man and Lazarus. They might have even witnessed Abraham and the rich man's conversation.

A few final questions about the Underworld, then I promise we'll move on. Didn't Abraham tell the rich man that no one can cross over the great chasm from the Hell side to the Paradise side and vice versa? If they couldn't move around the Underworld, how did Moses and Elijah leave Abraham's Bosom and join Jesus and the guys on Mount Hermon? You'll remember the rich man pleaded with Abraham to at least send Lazarus to his father's home to warn them of the torments of Hell. But Abraham said, "If they won't listen to Moses and the prophets, they won't listen even if someone rises from the dead." That statement says a lot but it does not say, "No, sorry, man. No one can leave Paradise and visit the living." Abraham did not say Lazarus was *unable* to go to the man's family. He said *he would not send him.* Interesting…

Let's rejoin the men on Mount Hermon. After witnessing the important conversation between Jesus, Moses, and Elijah, Peter exclaimed, "Rabbi, it's wonderful for us to be here! Let's make three shelters—one for you, one for Moses, and one for Elijah." He said this because he didn't really know what else to say, for they were all terrified. Then a cloud overshadowed them, and a voice from the cloud said, "This is my dearly loved Son. Listen to him." Suddenly, when they looked around, Moses and Elijah were gone, and they saw only Jesus with them. As they went back down the mountain, he told them not to tell anyone what they had seen until he had risen from the dead. So they kept it to themselves, but they often asked each other what he meant by "rising from the dead."[11]

My goodness! What a secret they had to keep. Not only did they experience the Shekinah glory exuding from Jesus as a taste of how He would appear once He received His glorified body, but they also met these colossally famous men of God! As you can see, Peter could identify the spirits of Moses and Elijah by sight because they appeared as physical human men. Otherwise, why would he think human spirits might need physical shelter?

And so, together, we have traveled the path on which the research took me to solve the mystery of where the spirits of Moses and Elijah came from when they joined their Messiah on Mount Hermon. But whatever happened to those righteous inhabitants of the Underworld's Paradise? Can they still come up from the Underworld? I'm so glad you asked! It's really the best part of the story, and because I *love* the way my husband tells it, I will let him do so:

For a moment, let's go back to the cross. We all know that Jesus died. "'Father, into your hands, I commit my spirit!' And having said this, He breathed His last."[12] But what happened after He died? We know His body was laid in Joseph's tomb, but what about His spirit? When Jesus died that day, the Bible tells us He went into the Underworld. He took the repentant man on the cross next to him to Paradise and the other man went to the place of torment called Hell.

How do we know Jesus went to Hades, and how long was He there? We know Jesus was there three days because He prophesied of Himself, "For as Jonah was in the belly of the great fish for three days and three nights, so will the Son of Man be in the heart of the Earth for three days and three nights."[13] Also, Psalm 16:10 says, "For you will not leave my soul in Sheol." Sheol is the Underworld. Later, Luke repeats the same verse in the book of Acts (2:27): "For you will not leave my soul in Hades."

The confusion comes from this because some think Hades and Hell are the same places. Some say Jesus went to Hell. Maybe you've even heard that. But we need to understand the Underworld because some in Satan's kingdom will say, "Well, it doesn't matter about this Jesus Christ. He went to Hell anyway," and they'll show you a scripture here where it uses the term Hades. Again, the confusion is with these two terms, and we need to understand: did Jesus go to Hades? Yes, because Hades means the Underworld. But did Jesus go to Hell? No, because Hell is the place of torment for those of the rebellion located in Hades/Underworld.

Jesus remained in the belly of the Earth for three days. Keep in mind that everybody who died on this Earth from the very beginning of time up to Calvary—Adam, Eve, Moses, David—all of those who were made righteous through following the Law, were in Paradise in the Underworld. Now all of a sudden, Jesus Christ the Messiah arrives in Paradise. Can you imagine what that must have been like? What was He doing down there for three days? Peter tells us, "For Christ also suffered once for sins, the just for the unjust, that He might bring us to God, being put to death in the flesh but made alive by the Spirit, by whom also He went and *preached to the spirits in prison*."[14] Jesus declared the good news and offered salvation to those who, in faith, awaited their Messiah in Abraham's Bosom/Paradise.[15]

But can you imagine what it was like on the Hell side of the chasm? They're in torment, and suddenly Paradise is so full of light and glory because God Himself is now in Paradise! And the penny is dropping in their minds. They understood who the Messiah was, all the Old Testament scriptures, and the things that the prophets said about the coming Messiah. Now there He is in the Underworld with them, close enough to see and hear, yet the chasm separates them.

After three days in Paradise, Jesus takes the keys of Hades (the Underworld), opens the prison doors, and all the saints in Paradise are released.[16] The Bible says, "When He ascended on high, He led captivity captive, and gave gifts to men." (Now this, "He ascended"—what does it mean but that He also first descended into the lower parts of the Earth? He who descended is also the One who ascended far above all the heavens, that He might fill all things.)[17]

So the resurrection of Jesus Christ is actually twofold. First, Father God raised Jesus from the dead. Second, when Jesus came up from the Underworld, He brought all the Old Testament saints who were waiting in Paradise with Him. Praise God! That's exciting because now Paradise in the belly of the Earth is closed. It's empty.

The Bible says that Jesus is the first fruits of the dead.[18] He's called the first fruits because He was the first brought to life, then He raised the rest of them with Him. Well, how do we know this? Because Matthew 27 (52-53) says, "and the graves were opened, and many bodies of the saints who had fallen asleep were raised; and coming out of the graves *after His resurrection*, they went into the holy city and appeared to many."[19] Now wouldn't you like to have been present in Jerusalem that day?

But, think for a moment about what's going on in Hell. I mean, the poor rich man—he's just having a bad day. One minute he's saying, "Oh, send Lazarus to at least give me some water. This is such a place of torment," and Father Abraham says, "no, we can't do that." And now Jesus shows up in Paradise, and the thirsty rich man sees Him. Imagine him leaning over to another of Hell's residents and saying, "Look over there. What's going on?" The Messiah comes, and he can hear the rejoicing, the singing, and the praise. He can hear different people quoting different prophecies from the Old Testament. And now those in Hell are realizing, "We've been duped! We've been lied to! Not only are those prophecies true, but there's the promised Messiah!" But I bet somebody in Hell is going, "No, this ain't real. Don't worry about it," because there's always a skeptic, right? Then Jesus takes the keys, opens the door, and sets all of them free. As the power of God brings Jesus, along with the resurrection of the saints, back up to the land of the living, all of a sudden, from Hell's view, Paradise is empty.

Wow! So, there's our answer! Today, human spirits cannot be called up from the dead because 2,000 years ago, Jesus emptied the only region of the Underworld where they could come from. But this story is not finished.

After Jesus was raised from the dead, He meets Mary at His tomb. As she's about to embrace Him, He says, "Don't touch me...."[20] A little over a week later, Jesus encounters His disciple Thomas and tells him to touch the wounds in His hands and side. Why did He invite Thomas to touch Him but forbid Mary? When He met Mary, He went on to say to her, "...I haven't yet ascended to the Father." However, when he saw Thomas, He had already gone to the Father. Why did ascending to the Father matter? Up to this point in Judaism's history, one of the most important responsibilities of an Old Testament high priest was once a year, he was given the privilege of offering an unblemished lamb sacrifice to atone for the sin of the entire nation. The lamb's blood was placed in a bowl, and the priest carried it into the tabernacle to the Holy of Holies. It's important to note that once he had that bowl in his hands, no one could touch him. Next, he sprinkled the blood on the Mercy Seat to atone for the people's sins. Once the blood was applied to the Mercy Seat and sin was covered (atoned for), he left the Holy of Holies and could be touched again. So Jesus had risen from the dead, and something happened between when He told Mary not to touch Him and when He told Thomas to touch Him.

What Jesus does between these two encounters is He stepped into His role as the "high priest of the greater and more perfect tabernacle not made with hands, that is, not of this creation. Not with the blood of goats and calves, but with His own blood He entered the Most Holy Place in the Third Heaven once and for all, having obtained eternal redemption."[21] All of Heaven is overjoyed—the Redeemer has arrived! He who gave up His place in Heaven and became flesh has now returned with His own blood to redeem the human race. The Father was probably bursting with pride that His son had finished the task. High Priest Jesus walks into the Holy of Holies, where the mercy seat is located, and sprinkles His blood on the Mercy Seat to eliminate sin from the human race as if it had never existed. The objects of God's affection are now redeemed! I can imagine there was a heavenly party like no other.

Jesus is rejoicing, but then He says, "I'm not done yet. Oh, but Father!

Look at everyone I brought with me." When Jesus was raised from the dead, all the people in Paradise in the Underworld were raised along with Him. The Apostle Matthew said that tombs opened, and the bodies of many godly men and women who had died were raised from the dead. They left the cemetery after Jesus' resurrection, went into the city of Jerusalem, and appeared to many people.[22] So when Jesus went to the third Heaven, the people he released from the Underworld were welcomed home to the present Paradise we now call Heaven.

Then, because of His great love for people, Jesus left that scene. He returned to Earth because He still had a few more days of discipleship to finish, a few more moments with His people, and a few more things to tell and teach them. Words like reach your finger here and look at My hands, and reach your hand here and put it into My side. Do not be unbelieving, but believing.[23]

Today, when redeemed Christ-followers die, we go directly to be with Jesus in Paradise in the Third Heaven.[24] Second Corinthians 5:8 says that to be absent from the body is to be present with the Lord. Before the cross, to be absent from the body meant to go to Abraham's bosom in the belly of the Earth. Notice anything different about the Underworld now?

The cross changed *everything!*

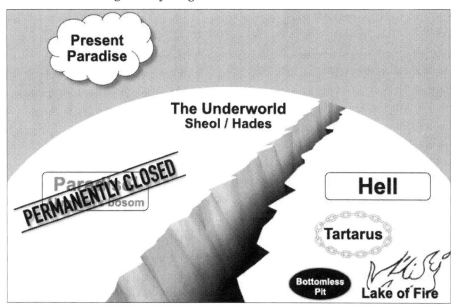

CHAPTER NINE

The Unrest of the Undead

"And I pray one prayer—I repeat it till my tongue stiffens—
Catherine Earnshaw, may you not rest as long as I am living!
You said I killed you—haunt me, then!...
Be with me always—take any form—drive me mad!
only do not leave me in this abyss, where I cannot find you!"
— *Heathcliff,* Wuthering Heights *(Brontë 153)*

Now we know that most humans go to either Hell in the Underworld or present-day Paradise in Heaven upon their death. But what prevents some of them from reaching their final destination?

The answer to this question is as varied and complex as each person's circumstances. As we just discovered, the cross changed everything about the afterlife. If a person is born again when their body dies, their spirit goes to be in the presence of our heavenly Father.[1] No limbo for them. However, if a person is not born again, there are several reasons they could be stuck, but each one requires a spiritual law to be activated. Most of those laws are embodied in the Ten Commandments. It is important to keep that in mind from this point on. (You may want to visit pages 64 and 65 to review them.)

Here are a few sins that can prevent a human spirit from passing on to their final resting place after the body dies. This is not a complete list.

Murder

To kill a human being unlawfully and with premeditated malice[2] is an act driven by a force. That force can be demons, hate, rage, fear, jealousy, or craving to possess a person, thereby killing them to be certain no one else can have them. Whatever the reason, murder is definitely a sin and the sixth of the Ten Commandments.[3]

Revenge

Also falling under the sixth commandment, revenge is an act of retaliating to get even for being hurt or harmed.[4] I've heard it said, "Before you embark on a journey of revenge, dig two graves!" Why? Because intending to destroy someone who has wronged us ultimately destroys us, too.[5] It holds a person in tremendous suffering. If the person was violently murdered, they might want their murderer tormented or brought to justice. Revenge also works with sexually or physically abused people when they are murdered. Though they are the victim, this person does not release the murderer of their wrongdoing and desires to satisfy their revenge.

Obsession

Socrates is credited with saying, "From the deepest desires often comes the deadliest hate." That quote perfectly defines the outcome of unbridled obsession and violates the second commandment (no idols). The literal definition is a persistent disturbing preoccupation with an often unreasonable idea or feeling.[6] When someone is genuinely obsessed, their interest has become compulsive, and they've begun to lose control over it. When they were living, this person may not have been able to let go of someone or something they love. This sounds sweet, but I'm not talking about a healthy, balanced kind of love. It is selfish and fear-centered. A perfect example of an obsessive relationship is that of Catherine and Heathcliff in Emily Brontë's *Wuthering Heights*.[7] After Catherine's death, her spirit wandered the moors, always seeking her lover, Heathcliff. Though Catherine is a fictitious character, her story is more realistic than most people understand.

Hatred

This person will not cross over because of their passionate hostility and hatred of a person. They manage to tick off five of the Ten Commandments: number two, maybe five, six, nine, and ten. In their lifetime, they exercised intense distasteful emotions for a person or people and mingled this with a feeling of ill will. They might have wished them disease, failure, or even death. Often, hatred and unforgiveness create a kind of quicksand for the soul and a miserable existence.

Violence

Often, suffering a violent death can hold a human spirit to this Earth. But how is a violent death that person's fault? Sometimes these legal rights do not seem fair! Well, this one is less simple to unpack, so stay with me here.

The first thing to keep in mind is that every human spirit that is "stuck" on the planet and does not move into the afterlife is a person who was spiritually dead upon their physical death. In other words, they were not born again. When people are spiritually dead, under God's Law delivered through Moses, they are also unclean. A verse in the Book of Numbers (19:20) helps explain why a person suffering a violent death can remain in limbo. "But the man who is unclean and does not purify himself, that person shall be cut off from among his people because he has defiled the sanctuary of the Lord. The water of purification has not been sprinkled on him; *he is unclean.*" There is a lot to be said about this verse, but the part that applies to a human spirit trapped on Earth is this:

1. That trapped person is unclean because of the condition of their spirit—it's dead.

2. To physically die in this condition means the spirit stays dead because they were unable to purify themselves—unable to become born again, spiritually alive.

3. When this verse says, "that *soul* (nephesh) shall be cut off from his people," it does not mean to be physically exiled. It means the punishment of spiritual death.[8]

Can human spirits read our minds?

No, they cannot read minds—they are, after all, human beings. But, they become skilled at predicting our behavior using what scientists call classical conditioning. The most famous example of classical conditioning involved the salivary conditioning of Ivan Pavlov's dogs. During his research on the digestion of dogs, Pavlov noticed that rather than simply salivating in the presence of food (the unconditioned response), the dogs began to salivate in the presence of the lab technician who usually fed them. Pavlov called these psychic secretions. In his initial experiment, Pavlov used a bell to call the dogs to their food, and after a few repetitions, the dogs started to salivate in response to the bell (the conditioned response). The sound of the bell became associated with food, causing the dogs to salivate.

The tactics a human spirit uses to condition us depend on the person's goal. If they are lonely and desire our company, they will not use scare tactics to force us into their presence. Instead, they may try to lure us in by gaining our trust. If they are spiteful and mean-spirited, they might use fear. For example, they know that if they make noise in a dark room just before entering it, we will eventually turn on the lights first. This seems like they read our minds about the light. However, it is simply a case of successful classical conditioning.

Can human spirits harm us?

The answer to this question is up to you. Are you seeking them out? Type "ghosts" into an internet search engine; the result is a list of about 1,800,000,000 sites.[9] That's a *lot* of interest. Type "ghost sightings" into the same search engine and find about 6,820,000 results.[10] There are hotels worldwide whose publicity revolves solely around ghosts who haunt their establishment. Some old towns offer midnight ghost tours. Of course, some cemeteries are famous today simply because of a particular spirit regularly spotted there.

If you actively pursue contacting a spirit, you will probably find one. But, unless you can see them, it will be difficult for you to know for sure if the spirit you meet is human or some other-worldly spirit.

In my experience, it can be dangerous to pursue contact, or even worse, a relationship with a human spirit or a demonic spirit. In the case of a human spirit, you cannot know what demons attend their way. If you seek them out, you open a spiritual door and give them access to you whenever and however they desire. Eventually, these encounters will bring distress and downright torment to your life! In a nutshell, the more you pursue any spirit, the more they can pursue you.

Do human spirits have a scent?

The kind of spirit that generates a scent when they are present is a demon called a familiar spirit. However, it is possible for a familiar spirit to be attached to a human spirit and then produce a scent when they are both present. When I was a child, I regularly smelled a sickeningly sweet perfume in my bedroom and accused my younger sister of spilling it on my carpet. She denied doing this so convincingly that I finally stopped searching the carpet for the smell. That's when I noticed the spirit of an older woman sitting on my bed. When she was present, her familiar spirit brought "her" scent—the sweet perfume.

Can human spirits fly?

They can "fly," but not like Casper the Friendly Ghost. A human spirit can appear by walking into a room and disappear by walking out of the room, just like any living creature. However, they can also appear out of thin air and disappear just as quickly.

Can human spirits haunt a place?

First, let's define the term haunt. According to *Merriam-Webster Dictionary*, it means "to frequent a place or appear to somebody in the form of a ghost or other supposed supernatural being."[11] Keep in mind that human bodies are physical containers for spirits. This means that even after the death of their body, a human spirit desires to fill a container. Also, human spirits have the same personality and habits as they did when their bodies were alive. This is why they are sometimes "stuck" in a physical location. The answer is yes; they can be attached to physical items such as buildings, dwellings, bones, blood, the spot where their body died, graves, idols, containers, garments or clothing, instruments of violence, and people to whom they had an obsessive attachment.[12]

Does the room get cold when human spirits are present?

Not always. Sometimes the hair on my arms or the back of my neck bristles in the presence of any spiritual entity. But it feels more like static electricity than a chill.

Can human spirits have sex with us?

No, they cannot have sex with us. This work is left to the Nephilim or a type of demon called incubus (male form) or succubus (female form). What are Nephilim, you ask? We're getting there.

Can we communicate with human spirits through Ouija boards, séances, or psychics?

As far back as 1100 BCE, the Chinese were the first to use "the talking board" to contact the dead and the spirit world. Also called Spirit Board or Witch Board, the basic Ouija board design hasn't changed since the beginning. It is a flat wood board marked with letters and numbers, and the words yes, no, maybe, goodbye, and other symbols. Participants place two to four of their fingers on a small heart-shaped piece of wood called a planchette, which then moves about the board to spell out words dictated by the spirit. Charles W. Kennard of the Kennard Novelty Company first marketed it as a board game in Baltimore, Maryland, in the early 1890s. Kennard gave it the name Ouija, which he believed to be the Egyptian word for luck. It isn't, but he claims the board told him this during a session, and the name stuck. Kennard Novelty Company sold it to Parker Brothers, who began selling the game in 1966.[13]

A séance is a meeting of people who have gathered to contact or receive messages from the spirit world—specifically human spirits. Often, a medium or psychic is present to make this contact possible. A psychic is a person sensitive to the spirit world who conducts readings for people. They are believed to be sensitive to spiritual forces and to possess extraordinary or mysterious perceptions or understanding of the spirit world. Most palm readers consider themselves psychics.

Now, to answer the question: *Can we communicate with human spirits through Ouija boards, séances, or psychics?* The answer is mostly yes, but let me qualify that answer. Usually, the spirits contacted with Ouija boards are demons. This is because human spirits need a human contact through whom to communicate, so the board game is not a good candidate. Most séances have a psychic present to speak on behalf of the spirit world. If the psychic is legitimate and not a con artist (most of them are), it is possible to contact a human spirit or another type of spirit posing to be human. Whether or not they are indeed the person you seek is a different story.

At the risk of belaboring a point, just about every person I've talked with who has seriously used Ouija boards, attended séances, or consulted psychics has developed spiritual problems one way or another. The Ouija board is a spiritual portal, and the demon that "owns" the board assigns a demon to the person asking questions of it. Consulting mediums and psychics establish soul ties (we'll talk about those later) with that person. Now their demons become your demons. Not a good situation if they have many of them! I'll teach you how to break the tie and free yourself from that person forever if you've already done this.

Can human spirits enter us?

Yes, human spirits can enter us.[14] The human body is designed to hold at least one human spirit. However, no spiritual law says it is limited to *only one* spirit.

One process is called the transference of spirits. This happens when one body exhales breath (remember, spirit means breath) and another body inhales that breath. Transference of human spirits is simply the passing of a life from one physical container to another. Jewish Kabbalah calls the spirit of a dead person who enters the body of a living person a *dybbuk*.[15] Many followers of Hinduism prefer the cremation of a corpse to prevent the spirit of the person from trying to re-enter their old body after death. They also believe some spirits may seek out human bodies in an attempt to fulfill their lusts and addictions. They call this *ghost possession* or *bhoots*.[16] High-ranking Satanists practice a special ceremony, usually just before they die, to transfer their human spirit and their demonic powers into another Satanist coming up in rank.

Methods to Transfer Human Spirits

There are three transference methods: One is when we willfully invite the spirit to enter us. Another is when we violate a moral law. The last is when we inherit human spirits because our ancestors violated a moral law.

1. By Invitation Only

A human spirit cannot accidentally transfer into us: we must invite them in. Some people who do this are called mediums. A medium becomes a channel of communication between the physical and the spiritual realm. Sometimes a medium sees a vision of the human spirit or hears them audibly, then repeats what the spirit says. Other times the spirit enters the medium and speaks through them. Some mediums are deceived by the spirit and invite them to remain inside. I have met others who invite them in because they believe it will give them greater spiritual power.

If you are a Christian, you might know the Old Testament story commonly referred to as The Witch of Endor. But I bet you haven't heard it explained like this.

Samuel the Seer was grieved when King Saul forfeited his crown due to his disobedience to God. He was so grieved that he did not see Saul again from that day until the day Samuel died. Sadly, Samuel was Saul's only connection to God. When Samuel died, Saul never heard from the Lord again.

When Saul's arch-enemy, the Philistines, advanced into the heart of Israel and encamped at Shunem, Saul brought all the armies of Israel together and encamped at Gilboa. From an elevation of 1,200 feet, King Saul would easily see the camp of the Philistines pitched upon the slopes of the opposite range at a distance of only about four miles. When Saul saw the Philistine army, he was so alarmed that his heart greatly trembled. But why was Saul so afraid? He had been victorious in his conflicts with the Philistines many times. Why would this time be any different? His great fear at the sight of the Philistine army can hardly be attributed to any cause other than the knowledge and feeling that God had forsaken him. He was suddenly overwhelmed and desperately needed God's help. He asked the Lord what he should do, but the Lord refused to answer him, either by dreams, sacred lots, or by the prophets.

Then Saul had an idea—a wonderful, awful idea. He told his advisers, "Find a woman who is a medium, so I can go and ask her what to do." Even though Saul had banned from the land of Israel all mediums and those who consulted the spirits of the dead, his advisers replied, "There is a medium at Endor." Fear and desperation have a way of driving us to do things we might never have considered before.

So Saul disguised himself by wearing ordinary clothing instead of his royal robes. Then he went to the woman's home in Endor at night, accompanied by two of his men.

"I have to talk to a man who has died," he said. "Will you call up his spirit for me?"

"Are you trying to get me killed?" the woman demanded. "You know that Saul has outlawed all the mediums and all who consult the spirits of the dead. Why are you setting a trap for me?"

But Saul took an oath in the name of the Lord and promised, "As surely as the Lord lives, nothing bad will happen to you for doing this."

Finally, the woman said, "Well, whose spirit do you want me to call up?"

"Call up Samuel," Saul replied, referring to his former friend and trusted prophet.

When the woman saw Samuel, she screamed, "You've deceived me! You are Saul, and you're trying to get me killed!"

"Don't be afraid!" the king told her. "What do you see?"

"I see a godlike spirit coming up out of the Earth."

"What does he look like?" Saul asked.

"He is an old man wrapped in a mantle."[17] Now Saul realized it was Samuel, and he fell to the ground before him.

"Why have you disturbed me by calling me up?" Samuel asked Saul.

"Because I am in deep trouble!" Saul replied. "The Philistines are at war with me, and God has left me and won't reply by prophets or dreams. So I have called for you to tell me what to do."

But Samuel replied, "Why ask me since the Lord has left you and has become your enemy? The Lord has done just as he said he would. He has torn the kingdom from you and given it to your rival, David.[18] The Lord has done this to you today because you refused to carry out his fierce anger against the Amalekites. What's more, the Lord will hand you and the army of Israel over to the Philistines tomorrow, and you and your sons will be here with me. The Lord will bring down the entire army of Israel in defeat." Immediately Saul fell full length on the ground and was dreadfully afraid because of the words of Samuel.[19]

What in the world? Is this one of those fictional allegorical stories meant to teach us a lesson? Some believe that is the case. Others believe the spirit that the medium called up was Satan disguised as Samuel. There are several theories and creative conclusions based on the confusing attributes of this story. So, why do I include it in this chapter if it's so confusing? Because it is a perfect example of what mediums do when they make themselves a communication channel between human spirits and the earthly realm.

Here's where the Rich Man and Lazarus story sheds some light (thanks to Jesus for leaving the breadcrumbs of revelation for us!). According to Underworld standard operating procedures, we know that because Samuel was a righteous man, he would have gone to Abraham's Bosom/Paradise in the Underworld upon his death. We further understand that departed spirits could leave and manifest on the Earth as long as they dwelt in Abraham's Bosom and not Hell. So Samuel could "come up" from the Underworld just as Moses and Elijah were called up by Jesus (functioning as a prophet) to chat with Him before He went to His crucifixion in Jerusalem.

We must understand that no spirit can come and go from the Underworld after Jesus released the righteous people from Abraham's Bosom and transported them to Paradise in the Third Heaven. The season of the ability to conjure spirits from the dead ended over 2,000 years ago. Suppose a present-day medium invites the spirit of a deceased human into them to communicate with their client. In that case, it's either a spirit trapped on the planet or an evil spirit impersonating the one called on.

In case you're curious about the conclusion of Saul's story, the Philistines did indeed attack Israel. Many were slaughtered on the slopes of Mount Gilboa when the Philistines closed in on Saul, and they killed three of his sons—Jonathan, Abinadab, and Malkishua. The fighting grew fierce around Saul, and the Philistine archers caught up with him and severely wounded him. Saul begged his armor-bearer to take his sword and kill him before the pagan Philistines came to run him through and torture him. But his armor-bearer was afraid and would not do it. So Saul took his sword and fell on it. When his armor-bearer realized Saul was dead, he fell on his sword and died beside the king. So Saul, his three sons, his armor-bearer, and his troops all died that same day.[20] Did Saul go to Abraham's Bosom? Did he go to Hell? Excellent questions with someday answers.

2. Violating a Moral Law

The second way a human spirit can enter is when we violate a moral law. Though the person may be ignorant of the transference, one of the most common ways it happens is during sex. Specifically, this would have to be an unmarried person having sex or a married person having sex with someone other than their spouse—more on this conversation later in the book. I have met a few human spirits who transferred into their rapists as their dying bodies exhaled their final breath. I have also talked to human spirits who, as they expired, entered their murderer's body.

3. Human Spirits Inherited Because our Ancestors Violated a Moral Law

A Goldi shaman[21] is chosen by an *ayami*, or spirit, that wields the power of the ancestral spirits. Listen to this shaman's description of the intimacy of this spirit contact, journey, and possession:

> "Once, I was asleep on my sick bed when a spirit approached me. It was a very beautiful woman… She said, 'I am the ayami of your ancestors, the shamans. I taught them shamaning. Now I am going to teach you.' She has been coming to me ever since, and I sleep with her as with my own wife, but we have no children… When I am shamaning, the ayami and the assistant spirits are possessing; whether big or small, they penetrate me as smoke or vapor would."[22]

Balinese Hinduism teaches that deceased ancestors can gain spiritual power and be involved in their descendants' lives. Spirits and ancestors are honored with offerings and housed in shrines or natural elements. They may affect every aspect of life, and, therefore, a complex apparatus of rituals and taboos is necessary to prevent an outbreak of calamities, diseases, deaths, and any other kind of adversity. On the whole, the Indonesian archipelago is characterized by folk tales, encounters with giants, and terrible creatures. No real distinctions between the living and the dead exist, and ever-present evil spirits inhabit even the bright green rice paddies of the islands.[23]

But the rest of us who are not shamans or Balinese Hindus also receive ancestral spirits through our families' generational lines. Whether we fully understand it or not, we have been influenced by the sins of ancestors we don't even know and most definitely by the sins and failures of our parents. For example, if the atmosphere of your home was one with much anger, you will likely have a hard time with anger in your own life. Or, if your parents brought pornography into the house, and even if you never knew about it, they opened the door to the activities of spirits of sexual lust and perversion that were free to torment them as well as you, their child. So, if your parents gave in to lust and sexual sin, you can understand why you might now find yourself struggling with those same things.

Many Christians have difficulty accepting this idea because of a specific Bible verse: But Christ has rescued us from the curse pronounced by the law. He took the curse for our wrongdoing upon himself when he was hung on the cross. It is written in the Scriptures, "Cursed is everyone who is hung on a tree."[24] However, this verse speaks to the condition of sin, not inherited bondage. Inherited spirits use the legal right provided by the Law, which says God assigns the punishment of the fathers upon the children to the third and fourth generations of those who hate Him.[25]

Even when we take care of the condition of sin by becoming born again, this does not automatically cleanse us from the spirits to whom our ancestors opened the doors. That process is accomplished by appropriating what Jesus did for us through His work on the cross. To appropriate is a fancy word that means to grab it as your own. Probably one of the most famous verses of the Bible is John 3:16, "For God loved the world so much that he gave his one and only Son so that everyone who believes in him will not perish but have eternal life." God doesn't want anyone to be destroyed,[26] and yet people die under the condition of sin and go to hell every day. If God so loved, then why are people perishing? Because they did not appropriate their redemption from sin. If I have applied that redemption to my spirit, I must also apply cleansing to the generational bondage in my soul.

PART 3

Soul Ties

CHAPTER TEN

When Innocence Expires

*"I am always drawn back to places where I have lived,
the houses and their neighborhoods."*
Truman Capote, Breakfast at Tiffany's

Like Mr. Capote, a distant train whistle draws me back to balmy July nights in my little hometown along the Mississippi River. The pungent scent of burning leaves recalls crisp autumn afternoons walking from school to my grandparents' house. The purr of a lawn mower motor conjures the sweet scent of fresh-cut grass wafting through my bedroom's white eyelet lace-covered window with the shade pulled halfway down. I am always drawn back to these places of innocence—places of comfortable ignorance.

Travel with me to a small village nestled in the Mississippi Valley. One side borders the river, another apple orchards and sprawling cornfields. My family has lived here nearly one hundred years now. Both of my mother's parents attended the same elementary and junior high school that both of my parents, four aunts, my little sister, some cousins, and I attended. My classmates are also my neighbors. In fact, many of their parents were my parents' neighbors. We have dwelled within the same two-mile radius of each other my entire life.

I will complete my first year of high school in only two months! My eighth-grade class village pond graduated fifty-two students. Then with both feet, I jumped into an ocean, a city high school of two thousand students. How exhilarating it is to swim in the sea.

A beautiful boy with thick black hair and long muscular legs runs hurdles on our junior varsity team at the track meet; for some reason, I haven't noticed him until now. After the race (Did he win or lose? I guess that bit of information isn't as important as the color of his eyes—*brown*.), the beautiful boy walks past me and turns back. His eyes glitter as he rolls them slightly sideways and says with an inviting expression, "Meet me in the foyer."

Fifteen minutes later, I sit beside him on a smooth wooden bench by the school's front door. I learned his name is Joel, which naturally sounds perfect when combined with my name—Joel and Denise. Melodious! For the next thirty minutes, we take turns offering each other morsels of ourselves in words, smiles, and sighs. I feel weightless and lovely.

Two months later, Joel tells me he loves me! He is the first one! The first one to whom I give my heart; the first one to whom I speak those three unhinging words, "I love you." I feel he completely accepts me for who I am, and I consider sharing my secret with him. He would be the first living human to whom I have ever confessed what I see. Yet I'm not sure he would still love me if he knew the truth about me, so I keep quiet.

We are together for three months before I finally give myself to him. It happens covertly, without fanfare, dark and cold, lying on an old musty mattress on my concrete basement floor. My innocence expires. I am fifteen years old.

What now? Well, *you can't un-ring the bell!* And *what's done is done!* is what my mother would say to me. She didn't, but it's what I would have told me if I were her. The reaming persists: I have ruined everything! Mom and Dad will be so disappointed in me! These derisory thoughts trample through my mind in the dark nights in my white princess bed in my purple room in my childhood home. The receding wail of a train whistle carried up from the river on the summer breeze filters through my eyelet curtains. It mocks my absent virginity recalling that it is a distant memory.

Just when the self-loathing and guilt feel as if they will overtake me, I see Joel again, and those familiar words drip languidly from his tongue—I love you. The world is made right again…at least for a little while.

Though I hardly noticed when it began, the spiritual atmosphere around me has undoubtedly shifted. I am aware of a spiritual entity that is much different from the beast. It is a heavy looming presence and seems to consume more space than logically possible. The air becomes dense as fog when the spirit settles in. At first, it appears in my room only at night when I am alone. Like a flock of timid birds, a smattering of less significant spirits constantly tags along after it. Of course, I deal with these spirits as I have skillfully learned to manage the others—I ignore them hoping they will just go away. They do not. The beast seems disinterested in all of them.

The eighteenth of each month is another anniversary of the blissful day we met. It is celebrated in the usual way—ten minutes of sex. Nine months have passed, and I am age sixteen now. I'm beginning to feel that Joel might discard me if there isn't a constant and ready supply of sex. The whispered rumors I overhear at school that he is sleeping with several other girls support this theory. He doesn't say he loves me often now. I stoop to regularly asking him, "Do you still love me?" to be answered brusquely with, "Of course. I'm still here, aren't I?" What girl wouldn't be reassured by that? I'm beginning to feel like I'm sinking and have nothing to grasp onto.

Even though some might describe our relationship as having deteriorated, I feel I hold one powerful trump card in my proverbial pocket—Joel's mother loves me. She has drawn me closely into her heart, which is where I feel safe. I sense a new strength coursing through me when I am with her, and I regularly stop after school to see her when no one else is home. She is always welcoming and reassuring. She promises he doesn't love the other girls and educates me on the concept that young men need to sow their wild oats to stay satisfied. She says I will always have his heart; even if he strays, he will never stray too far. I believe her, and we form an alliance.

The heavy looming presence is with me night and day now. Rather than feeling frightened by it, peculiarly, I feel I can trust it. In fact, it is somewhat useful to have around. If my boyfriend goes missing (he is prone to doing this regularly), then the presence makes me "aware" of his location. And by aware, I mean it informs me of the girl's name and phone number where he can be reached. On one occasion, I am daring enough to call her house and ask to talk to him. This tactic seems to have quickened a surge of self-control in Joel, preventing him from sleeping around for at least a dozen-plus days. It was many years before I understood the destructive influence the presence had on my life.

Naturally, plans to be married right after high school are plotted by our first anniversary. His mother and I are thrilled. I am all that she has ever hoped for in a daughter-in-law. I am closer to her than any of her daughters—it is a perfect scenario. However, I am aware that my fiancé is not as excited as we are.

I imagine that if we stop having sex, I will probably start to feel better about myself, my life, and who I have become. I try this approach with my fiancé, who plays along for a while but only becomes angry and distant in the end. Of course, the sex begins again; not that it had stopped, it had only just paused. I begin to feel increasingly depressed and vacant. By my own choice, I've secluded myself from most of my friends and feel a deep loneliness when I'm not with Joel—or his mother.

My spiritual entourage is constantly growing, which aids my difficulty in sleeping at night. Just as I dose off, I am awakened by, "Where could he be?" whispered in my ear. A great panic grips me. It's true—I don't know where he is! Rather than being at home in bed, he could be in the arms of any unsuspecting virgin. "You could lose him! What would you do without him?" the snippety demon stabs fear like the goading tip of a knife into my heart. As soon as I turn to the presence, it engulfs me, and the fear immediately ceases.

"Don't worry. He's in our hands," it lies convincingly to soothe my distress. The spirit's words move through me like smoke filters through the spaces of a room, and it warms me on the inside. Its darkness doesn't seem quite as looming as before.

My thoughts become obsessed with Joel. Meanwhile, the pithy demons trailing the presence incessantly wheeze in my ears, forming their sentences in the first person as if they are my thoughts. Presumably, they do not realize I can see them. Or if they do, they are just that stupid. "He is beautiful; how did I ever get him? If he leaves me, I will die! Who will ever want me now? Used! Tramp! Whore!" they chide, weaving their words like a thick, wet blanket.

When I'm with Joel, they take a different course. "Is he flirting with her? If only I were thinner, he would never look at another girl. I bet he hates the sound of my voice. If I were blond, he would love me." These thoughts come in rapid-fire sequence most of the time. Just when it becomes unbearable, the presence swallows them up within its black hole of non-space. This always silences them, and I am grateful for the presence. It is a dwelling place of comfortable ignorance.

Another anniversary passes before the inevitable break-up occurs. He tells me that I feel more like a sister to him than a girlfriend. He's just not attracted to me "that way" anymore—biting words branded into my heart. His mother can do nothing to convince him otherwise. She died the following year, and my heart was wrenched.

For years, I yearned for Joel. I caught glimpses of him around corners. His voice jolted my heart in strangers' conversations. There were nights filled with sweet lingering dreams of him. One night his spirit appeared in my room and cajoled me not to be sad, that he would remain with me no matter where I went. And he did.

CHAPTER ELEVEN

Dissever My Soul

And neither the angels in Heaven above
Nor the demons down under the sea
Can ever dissever my soul from the soul
Of the beautiful Annabel Lee
Edgar Allan Poe, "Annabel Lee"

No matter how casual we might think sex is, it is critically important to the spirit world. In fact, sex is the fastest way for spirits to acquire new real estate. Interested?

The topic of sex can be sensitive, and experience warns me that discussing it could stir up some angry feelings. This could be another spot you might even decide to trash this book! Talking about sex has often provoked a negative response from those I have counseled, but my intent is not to offend you or ruin your fun. Because this book is about what I see, I will share what happens in the spirit realm when we have sex with someone we are not married to.

Even though my personal story is dramatic, I realize not everyone's first sexual encounter is depressing. Each person is unique, and what might be a failure for one may be a sweet memory for another. Because of this, I would like to avoid focusing on the emotional aspect of my experience. Instead, let's use it to observe the spirit world's rules and rights concerning sex. These are some common questions I'm asked.

What is the definition of sex?

Today, what counts as sex has blurred lines. I have had conversations with people of all ages about what they believe sex is or is not. Many define it by what they think it is not. They say it is *not* sex if one of these points is true:

- Ejaculation occurs outside rather than inside the body.
- Intercourse is anally rather than vaginally.
- Ejaculation or orgasm occurs through oral or physical stimulation.
- One or both partners do not achieve orgasm.
- Condoms are used.
- Objects, rather than body parts, are used for penetration.

Soren Kierkegaard said, "There are two ways to be fooled. One is to believe what isn't true; the other is to refuse to accept what is true." One statement I cannot repeat enough is this: what people believe is the truth is irrelevant to demons, and our ignorance of the rules is always an advantage to them. With that in mind, we invite the spirit world into our lives through sexual relationships when at least *one* of the following occurs:

- Physical penetration of *any* kind.
- Ejaculation or orgasm is achieved by *any* method.

These actions do not need to be consensual between the two parties. Demons just do not care about our feelings when it comes to consent. They also do not care if we are in love with our partner—love is not a get-out-of-jail-free card. The sexual act between people is of utmost importance to demons.

What spiritually happens to us when we have sex?

We discussed that we are made up of three parts: body, soul, and spirit. Our bodies are involved when we have sex, but the mind, emotions, and will also are engaged, creating a connection—a *soul tie*. This soul tie is an invisible spiritual connection that fastens our soul to our sexual partner's soul.

There's an ancient story that illustrates this soul connection. A young Hebrew woman named Dinah went out to visit the local women of the land of

Canaan, where Dinah's family resided. When Shechem, a Hivite prince who ruled Canaan, saw her, he raped her. The original text says that after he raped her, "Shechem's soul clave unto Dinah."[1] Well, that's a super word. What does *clave* mean? In Hebrew, the word clave is *dabaq*[2] and means to be joined together. Shechem and Dinah's souls were joined together by a sexual soul tie.

Some call soul ties between lovers psychic connections or cords. One website writes, "A psychic connection, or psychic link, is a spiritual connection between two people that transcends physical boundaries."[3] This is because when we have sex with someone we are not married to, demons have the legal right to access our souls through soul ties.

How do demons use soul ties?

A crude thing some people say when they have sex with someone is, "I got a piece of that!" Unfortunately, that is precisely what happens. When we have sex, the piece of our soul we give to a partner is prime real estate to their demons and establishes a spiritual connection between our souls. So here's the part that is critically important to understand. Demons that control one person's soul use the soul tie as their passageway to the other person's soul. They can easily move back and forth between the two carrying with them more demons to deposit.

You'll remember in my story how the spiritual atmosphere around me shifted after I had sex with my boyfriend. This is because a soul tie was established. Just as I am not aware when my brain communicates with my heart to cause it to beat, I was unaware a spiritual link had been made between my soul and his soul. The more sexual partners Joel acquired, their demons became his demons, which then became *my* demons. I grew more miserable with each new sexual experience he had. The soul tie between us not only informed me of his new sexual experiences, but the new demons he acquired made their way to me.

Here's another example of how soul ties work. I met with a young woman I hadn't seen for several months. I immediately became aware of her new soul tie because I could see it and the multitude of "new" demons trailing behind her. After chit-chatting for a little while, I said, "So, who are you having sex with?"

Looking shocked and feigning a hurt expression, she said, "No one! I'm not having sex. I'm *still* a virgin."

"Don't try to tell me you're not having sex. You know I can see your soul tie," I replied.

After a bit more resistance, she explained she wasn't having sex because he wasn't ejaculating inside her. Of course, we've already established that any physical penetration creates a soul tie, and demons are not concerned with our belief system. As we talked a little more, she confessed she was struggling with bouts of depression which was new for her. I wasn't surprised because I knew her boyfriend was addicted to heroin, and his demons of depression had become her demons of depression.

What legal rights do demons exercise to use soul ties?

Here's another super word we can talk about: *fornication* (I swear I'm not as old as I sound). My fight for freedom has taken me down some interesting paths, but I first learned about sexual soul ties in the Cleansing Seminar more than 30 years ago. By then, the damage had been done, and I had a long list of names of people to whom my soul clave unto.

Depending on your religious background, you might have heard of fornication. It means illicit or unlicensed sexual intercourse,[4] and the Bible says don't do it. First Corinthians 6:18 is only one of 36 times fornication is mentioned in the Bible. The author warns, "Flee fornication! No other sin so clearly affects the body as this one does. For sexual immorality is a sin against your own body." So, what's the big deal? Why is that a sin if two people want to have consensual sex? No one is getting hurt, are they? Besides exchanging demons, a seriously important reason to avoid fornication is that it affects our relationship with God. Though the church in Corinth existed almost 2,000 years ago, their problems were not much different from ours today. They had many issues, but all stemmed from one: the people could not or would not detach themselves from the world they lived in.

Corinth was the home of the temple of Aphrodite or Artemus, the goddess of sensual love and pleasure. It's been said that one thousand temple prostitutes served at her temple. Even in the morally corrupt society of the Roman Empire, Corinth was known for its excessive moral decay. The Romans used the word "Corinthian" in a derogatory way for someone who was immoral and excessive in that immorality. Corinth was sin city, the "Las Vegas" of the Roman Empire.[5] This is why Paul wrote in his first letter to the church in Corinth, "Don't you realize that your bodies are actually parts of Christ? Should a man take his body, which is part of Christ, and join it with a prostitute? Never! And don't you realize that if a man joins himself with a prostitute, he becomes one body with her? For the Scriptures say, 'The two are united into one.' But the person who is joined to the Lord is one spirit with him."[6]

Sex outside of marriage does double damage. It creates a soul connection that spirits use to pass between partners, and it harms my relationship with Christ.

Are there other kinds of soul ties?

Even though my personal story illustrates a sexual soul tie, there are several other kinds of soul ties, and the spirit world uses them just the same. I have seen a soul tie created between two people when needles are involved because any physical penetration makes a soul tie. This works between the giver and receiver of body piercings, tattoos, anesthesia, acupuncture, and even surgery.

Soul ties that are not necessarily evil are formed when people enter into covenants. Covenant? Isn't that kind of an ancient biblical term? Yes and no. The word covenant is used throughout several bibles, but it's also used in present-day society. The definition of covenant is an agreement or promise between two or more parties to engage in or refrain from a specified action.[7] Currently, there are covenants used in real property law, restrictions set on contracts (Covenants, Conditions, and Restrictions - "CC&Rs"), racial covenants (residential segregation), and many others, including blood covenants.

Blood covenants are not fictitious campfire stories told by bullies attempting to frighten other children. Blood covenant ceremonies have been practiced for centuries by primitive and modern people alike, and they are governed by a spirit that binds the souls together. In his book, *The Blood Covenant*,[8] H. Clay Trumbull tells the story of two young Lebanese men as they perform the rite of blood-covenanting.

> They had known each other and had been intimate for years, but now they were to become brother-friends in the covenant of blood. Their relatives and neighbors were called together in the open place before the village fountain to witness the sealing compact. The young men publicly announced their purpose and their reasons for it. Their declarations were written down, in duplicate, on one paper for each friend and signed by themselves and by several witnesses. One of the friends took a sharp lancet and opened a vein in the other's arm. Into the opening thus made, he inserted a quill through which he sucked the living blood. The lancet blade was carefully wiped on one of the duplicate covenant papers. Then it was taken by the other friend, who made a like incision in its first user's arm and drank his blood through the quill, wiping the blade on the duplicate covenant record. The two friends declared, "We are brothers in a covenant made before God: who deceiveth the other, him will God deceive." Each blood-marked covenant record was then folded carefully, to be sewed up in a small leather case, or amulet about an inch square; to be suspended about the neck or bound upon the arm, in token of the indissoluble relationship. As it is the comingling of their lives, nothing can transcend it.

Soul ties occur between two or more people when they join fraternal organizations or secret societies such as Freemasonry or college fraternities and sororities. This is because these organizations require members to take an oath that creates a covenant. This implies that the members agree to the organization's rules, sometimes including secrets that outsiders are not privy to. As is the case with Freemasonry, these can consist of blood covenants.

Speaking of covenants, some dark crafts carry out ceremonial covenants to form soul ties expressly to gain power. Santeria, Palo or Palo Mayombe (also known as Las Reglas de Congo),[9] Voodoo, Hoodoo, Druidism, Wicca (a descendant of Druidism), Satanism, and witchcraft are just a few that observe ceremonies to create soul ties intentionally. If one person they aim to control is not physically present, they will use that person's hair, saliva, blood, semen, skin, fingernail or toenail clippings, teeth, or bones. How can this work? It works because each item contains that person's identity—their DNA (deoxyribonucleic acid).[10] DNA is hereditary material in humans and all living organisms. Just about every cell in a person's body has the same DNA unique to them. Though DNA does not provide us with someone's soul information, it does connect demons to their body and soul.

Can evil spirits pass through soul ties between family or friends?

Yes and no. Evil spirits pass through soul ties if immoral behavior is involved in the relationship. Immoral behavior includes abuse, illegal activity performed together, unforgiveness, hatred, etc. But when the relationship is healthy, we are strengthened by love, loyalty, and support through the soul tie.

* * *

I realize this seems extreme and unfair. That's because it is! Remember, evil spirits' plans are to steal, kill, and destroy everything good in our lives.[11] They are legalistic and they are not geared to "play fair." I hope you're still interested.

PART 4

Nephilim

CHAPTER TWELVE

The Secret Garden

I come here late in the afternoon as the cool begins to settle in. It is a densely shaded spot where the ground is damp, smooth, and thrills the soles of my feet. Lingering in this place is tempting because it's still and tension-expelling. However, the promise of seeing *him* again is what draws me—not the bait of paradise.

True to his word, he appears again, and his lips pleasantly turn up at the corners when he sees me. Sun pooled in shafts catch in his hair and change the color of the Spanish moss from gray to green, gray to green. He is magical.

He clasps my hand and asks, for possibly the zillionth time, *Please go with me?* to which I have whispered *No* each time—each time but this one. He holds me silently, and the quiet expresses more than lovely words could ever accomplish. "Now that's enough," I say, though I believe it is not. It's just that after an hour in his arms, my twenty-year-old heart begins to feel as if it will burst. Eventually, he releases me, and we step onto a wisteria-sheltered path.

However, I've never ventured this far. I've usually whispered my final *No* by now; he has chivalrously raised my hand to his lips, kissed it sweetly, smiled reassuringly, and called for one of his assistants to escort me back to the meeting place. This time is different.

Reason would compel me to be apprehensive, though I feel only calm, peaceful, and secure in his presence—no beastie in sight. The many intertwined paths lead one to another, twisting this way and that. I could not find my way to the meeting place now if I tried, but I don't mind. It has become too narrow for us to travel side by side, so I step in behind him, adapting to his comfortable pace. He leads me in this solitary way for many moments before entering a clearing.

Suddenly, we are not alone. This area is humming with people passing through three or four intersecting trails. Everyone says Hello or nods to him, and it becomes evident to me now that each one knows the other; surprisingly, they seem to recognize me, too. I am sure I have never met anyone here, but there is something vaguely familiar about each one.

"We're almost there; can you see it?" he says as if we are approaching the Great Pyramid of Giza. The scene ahead soon reveals a sparkling ivory-colored tower built into the side of a mountain. As we approach, I see it is ornately decorated with bleached woodcarvings of vines and flowers inlaid with precious gems of all kinds. This stunning staircase is paved with layers of Mother of Pearl and leads ever upward. Waterfalls passing through the tower's winding vines create a muffled jingle. It is difficult to determine if the rocks and waterfalls have permeated the tower or if the tower is built around the rocks and waterfalls. It is breathtaking!

We leisurely climb the tower together. Those ascending or descending the grand staircase step aside, allowing us to pass. Each level displays tranquil lounging areas draped in colorful fabrics and posh pillows. I hear something resembling wind chimes, or could it be the breeze passing through the woodcarvings? A faint scent of lilacs rests in the air, and I think to myself, *I am saturated with peace to the core of my being.*

He leads me into a concealed space like a grotto carved into a mountain. It's cool, and the stone floor refreshes my bare feet stinging from the ascent. I shiver: not with cold but with enthusiasm. In this place, we are entirely secluded from inquiring eyes and have only each other to focus on. I'm happy to be done with the journey, and a warm stillness etherizes me. Sensing this, he invites me to recline on an overstuffed pillow bed. What was that? "Did I just hear distant thunder?" I purr. Of course, that would be quite out of character for this practically perfect scenario, but he laughs it off. This is the first check that he doesn't know me as well as I had initially believed. If he did, he would have known how welcoming and calming thunder is to my soul.

His movements are cautious to this point, though once I am relaxed and distracted with the serene accouterments, without warning, he transforms into a ravenous animal! Suddenly my clothes are snatched off, and the full weight of his body is upon me, crushing me into the bed. Anesthetized by some bewitching unseen power, I cannot move or breathe! Then with great force, he thrusts himself inside of me. His touch now feels like a burning all through me, as though I have touched fire. His voice trails to a mere moth of sound even as the light around me grows increasingly dim—I am losing consciousness.

A train whistle blows long. What? A train whistle? Suddenly I feel an upward surge as if out of deep water when you are about to lose the only breath left inside your lungs. *Denise, wake up.* I hear myself screaming. *Wake up!* Though each smell, sound, touch, and sight seemed real, it suddenly occurs to me that I have been asleep this entire rendezvous. As if my life depends on it, I force my eyes open. I am stunned to discover that my dream companion is there, physically upon me and inside me! However, now I am not dreaming, and his face changes before my eyes as he transforms into an elongated disproportionate manlike creature. I can gasp for air now but am still unable to speak or move at all. He remains writhing in me until, at last, he has accomplished his sexual claim.

From that moment to fifteen years after, there were no inviting dreams to lure me into his arms. He would wait until I was asleep, impose some supernatural trance, then enter me. I would awaken but was mute and paralyzed. I could not get away from his grasp, his touch, his body on me and in me. I could not whisper a sound, nor could I barely breathe. He simply exited when he finished, leaving me to my silent tears. I was his prisoner, his possession, at his mercy. All because of the one time in the garden when I did not say no.

* * *

Dreams are far more than a fairy tale wish your heart makes. In his short story *Master Misery*, Truman Capote described them this way: "Dreams are the mind of the soul and the secret truth about us." They can reveal mysteries about our subconscious soul *and* the spirit world's interaction with us. For years, I believed I was dreaming about the man in the garden. Not until he raped me did I force myself to awaken from his dreamlike coma and catch him in the act. At last, I realized what I was experiencing was much more than a dream—in reality, it was an evil spirit sexually violating me.

It would take numerous pages in small print to list the people I know who have had sexual experiences with spiritual beings. It is so common that hundreds of these stories can be found on the internet just by typing into a search engine *sex with demons* or *sex with spirits*. Some folks are tormented by their experiences; others welcome them. There are even websites that give you step-by-step instructions on how to invite a spirit to have sex with you. If you are contemplating this, please take my advice and *do not do it*. This is a dangerous path to pursue. If you have already had sex with a spirit, or if a spirit has had sex with you against your will, I hope what follows will help you understand what you have experienced.

CHAPTER THIRTEEN

Giants In the Land

*And as it was in the days of Noah,
so it will be also in the days of the Son of Man.*
Luke 17:26

In the past, the subject of sex with the supernatural world was confusing to me, but that's because there were specific details I had overlooked. If you see what I see, you may have noticed that different kinds of spirits have sex with people. One type is fallen angels (sometimes called watchers), and the other is Nephilim. Yes, we are *finally* going to talk about Nephilim. Since fallen angels have been around a lot longer than Nephilim, we'll talk about them first.

I have described two classifications of spirits: Class One gains power only by becoming bound to a human. Class Two has no desire to be bound to human souls because their responsibility is to influence the spirit world around people. Fallen angels that have sex with people belong in Class One. This spirit's power is limited by the amount of control it has over the person to whom it is joined. The more times it has sex with the person, the more power it has over them. Eventually, the watcher wields so much control that it can manifest through the human personality, seemingly against the person's will. But fallen angels have a dual purpose. Not only are they able to become bound to a human soul, but they are also assigned to locations to guard and protect spiritual high places. These locations are spiritually charged because humans have performed sinful actions in order to usher in spiritual control. This subject deserves an entire book to be written about it, so for now, I will leave it at that.

Another kind of spirit that performs sexual acts with humans is in the therion category—*incubus* and *succubus*. Merriam-Webster Dictionary defines an incubus as an evil spirit believed to lie upon a person in their sleep, especially to have sexual intercourse with women.[1] It defines a succubus as a spirit assuming female form to have sexual intercourse with men.[2] While these definitions are a bit simplistic, they are pretty accurate.

On the other hand, Nephilim do appear and act humanlike. Here are some questions that I'm regularly asked about them and what I have learned over the last two decades. I hope this information will help you understand what you see and how Nephilim are set apart from every other spiritual creature.

What are Nephilim?

The Nephilim topic is not new. Some say Nephilim were Neanderthals that inexplicably died out 28,000 years ago. Others believe they are present-day superhuman war soldiers hidden by the government for the last world battle, after which they will usher in the New World Order. I need a tall glass of water because that one's a big pill to swallow! My understanding of Nephilim is grounded in the past and the present. I understand them as supernatural beings with human souls (mind, will, emotions), human features, and fallen angel spirits. However, there once was a time when they also had physical bodies.

The first historical account of Nephilim is found in Genesis 6:4, "There were giants (*Nephilim*) on the Earth in those days, and also afterward, when the sons of God came into the daughters of men and they bore children to them. Those were the mighty men who were of old, men of renown."

This ancient text, originally written in Hebrew, can be challenging to interpret. Learning the meaning of specific phrases will help us understand the message. First, let's look at the *sons of God (ben Elohim)* expression. Throughout the Old Testament, this title refers to *spiritual beings created directly by God*, not born through humans. It applies to only two types of creations. One type is angels, which we've talked about several times. The Bible makes it clear that a special act of God created angels. Psalm 148:2, 5 says, "Praise Him, all His angels…*for He commanded and they were created.*" They did not evolve from a previous life form. They did not originate on some other planet. God, Himself created them.

According to the Bible, the second type of spiritual being created directly by God was Adam, the first human being. "So God created man *in His own image*; in the image of God He created him; male and female He created them."[3] We discussed this earlier in the book.

The sons of God angels referenced in Genesis 6:4 weren't the same as the Book of Psalms angels—they were insubordinate angels. We could even call them mutinous. "So the great dragon was cast out, that serpent of old, called the devil and Satan, who deceives the whole world; he was cast to the Earth, and his angels were cast out with him."[4] To clear up any confusion, the great dragon, the serpent of old, and the devil are different names for the same being—Satan. Sidebar: An interesting study for another day is later in the Book of Revelation it says this same great dragon gives to the beast (therion) his *power* (super strength to do miracles), *authority* (positional power), and his *throne* (judgment seat).[5] The great dragon is allowed by God to delegate his attributes, possessions, and spiritual authority to whom he wills. Interesting. When these deceived angels gave their allegiance to Satan and rebelled with him against God, they became the great dragon's messengers on Earth.

Now, let's look at the phrase, *daughters of man*. After God created Adam, man created all other human life. "And Adam lived one hundred and thirty years, and begot a son *in his own likeness*, after *his image*, and named him Seth."[6] In Hebrew, a male descendant of a man is referred to as a son of man (*ben 'adam*), and a female descendant of a man is referred to as a daughter of man (*bath 'adam*).

Putting this into context, we can say that a son of God is a being of Godly origin, and a daughter of man is a woman of human origin. Now the meaning of Genesis 6:4 is a bit clearer. When it says, "the sons of God came in to the daughters of men, and they bore children to them," it means rebellious angels physically manifested and had sex with human women. Our next question should be, who were the children born to the women?

Typical of this style of Hebrew literature, the first part of this verse states who the children were, and the last part repeats it as a conclusion. "*There were giants on the Earth* in those days, and also afterward, when the sons of God came in to the daughters of men, and they bore *children* to them. *Those were the mighty men who were of old, men of renown.*" The writer uses three terms to identify the same creations: children, mighty men, and giants. In Hebrew, the word giants is Nephilim. So Nephilim are the physical offspring of fallen angels and human women.

The great Romano-Jewish historian Flavius Josephus (37–100 AD) wrote, "For many angels of God accompanied with women, and begat sons that proved unjust, and despisers of all that was good, on account of the confidence they had in their own strength; for the tradition is, that these men did what resembled the acts of those whom the Grecians call giants."[7]

You may wonder how these ancient giants bring us to the Nephilim we see today. Because if you see what I see, then you also realize Nephilim are spiritual creatures who do not currently have physical bodies. Which begs the question, what happened to their bodies?

The story continues in Genesis 7:21. It tells us: "*Every living thing* that moved on the Earth *perished*—birds, livestock, wild animals, all the creatures that swarm over the Earth, and all mankind." Every living thing would also include Nephilim, for they had physical bodies then. What caused every living thing to perish? We know it today as Noah's Great Flood. Okay, I am not going to debate whether or not this was a local flood or a worldwide flood. The scientific fact is that there *was* a great flood. A Washington Post article titled "Artifacts Found In the Black Sea May Be Evidence Of A Biblical Flood"[8] stated this: "Archaeologists said yesterday they have discovered the remains of a manmade structure more than 300 feet below the surface of the Black Sea, providing dramatic new evidence of an apocalyptic flood 7,500 years ago that may have inspired the Biblical story of Noah." Noah and the Nephilim would have lived near present-day Iran, close to the Black Sea. Therefore, it is believable that the flood of 5500 BCE is the flood that destroyed every living thing that moved on the Earth during Noah's time.

Just as a human spirit is released into the spiritual realm when their body dies, the same is true for the Nephilim of old. When their physical bodies drowned in the great flood, their demonic spirits with human souls were released into the spirit world. This brings us back to my original description of Nephilim: they are supernatural beings with human souls and evil spirits. Their only desire is to inhabit a physical body, which is why they pursue a variety of human relationships.

What do Nephilim look like?

Whereas demons look like animals, reptiles, birds, or monsterish combinations of these creatures, Nephilim look far more human. The difference between Nephilim and human appearance is that the features of Nephilim are exaggerated in some way. They may be incredibly tall with gangly arms and legs, or their facial features could be disproportionate. Certain body parts are exaggerated depending on their particular "job description." For example, I once saw a Nephilim that motivated deviant sexual acts through the human to whom they were bound. Take a gander at which part of its body was abnormally large. This giant had an enormous erect penis that proudly waved about three feet tall. It was disgusting!

What do Nephilim do?

Demons are sinister, calculating, and cold, with no ability to experience emotion other than anger and hatred. I'm not sure that's actually an emotion when it comes from them; more like a force. On the other hand, Nephilim can identify with human emotion because they are spiritual offspring of humans. They can mimic human emotions and thoughts because they have human feelings and thoughts.

Half of your DNA comes from your mother, and half comes from your father. Similarly, you can say Nephilim have half-human DNA and half-angel DNA. They interpose easily between the two. Fallen angels are intelligent beings who have studied human behavior throughout time but are incapable of experiencing human emotions. So, they cooperate with Nephilim to accomplish human control on a much deeper emotional level than they could do by themselves.

We have encountered beings that manifest like a demon at first, yet, as the battle continues, you feel they are "bigger." Bigger in the sense that everything is exaggerated—emotionally and mentally. They control more of the person than a regular demon can. And most of all, they resist with a "bigger" tenacity. Nephilim prey on human emotions to coerce a person into a relationship. As was demonstrated in my personal experience, they can be attractive and incredibly seductive. But, when resisted, they will change their appearance to become more intimidating, and they become brutal. They capitalize on feelings of loneliness, hopelessness, sadness, loss, fear, anger, rage, and pleasure. Eating disorders and any addiction will involve Nephilim.

The quickest way for Nephilim to gain control of a person is through traumatic events. This is not a complete list, but these events include:

- Rape, physical, sexual, mental and/or emotional abuse.
- Death of a significant person.
- Acute rejection or abandonment.
- Near-death experience.
- Sex with Nephilim.

Symptoms of Nephilim control are when emotions acquainted with these events feel out of control, "over the top." These events don't have to lead to Nephilim control, but from hundreds of conversations with people who have experienced Nephilim activity in their lives, I've discovered they are the most common ones.

***

A lot has been written about Nephilim. There are reams of questionable literature stating as fact how they came to exist, what their purpose is, and a host of other conflicting information. However, not much has been written about what they are today—at least not spiritually. Don't be duped into believing they are aliens from other planets and that we should make them feel at home with us. They aren't superhumans with extraordinary intelligence and strength cooperating with the U.S. government for future wars. There are many more bizarre ideas you'll read and hear about Nephilim. I expect these ideas to become even more outlandish as time goes on.

I also believe there are physical Nephilim already coexisting with us. Sex with the spirit world has become more common and acceptable. One woman said, "I used to have visits from spirits and have sex with them. It was very pleasurable. It was almost like a real relationship with a guy."

Another woman described how she longed for a closer relationship with Jesus Christ. Then one night, a male spirit appeared to her, and he said he was Jesus. He told her how much he loved her and that she belonged to him. He knew things about her that no one else knew. He visited her almost every night for weeks until one night, he told her if she truly loved him, she would allow him to have sex with her—so she did. She had sex with him for hours, many nights in a row. This went on for a few more weeks until he transformed his penis into a knife, began cutting her female parts, and physically abused her. When she told him to stop, he became even more aggressive. He wouldn't leave her alone! She came to us for a soul-cleansing, and we helped her cut spiritual ties with him. Then we cast out Nephilim "Jesus"! To this day, that giant has never returned to her.

PART 5

Authority & Subjection

CHAPTER FOURTEEN

Spirit Voices

The banyan tree is what captures my attention. It is the most peculiar tree I've ever seen. They certainly don't grow them like this along the Mighty Mississippi's banks. This tropical fig is grander than any one of its epiphytic relatives. I suppose this particular tree stands ninety to a hundred feet tall—it is *enormous*. Glossy green leaves decorate the massive limbs, and aerial prop roots descend from them into the rich soil to become new trunks. From a distance, this old banyan resembles a dreadlocked human head emerging from the ground. It is only a five-minute walk from Villa Dianna, our island paradise vacation home.

Once I go beyond admiring the tree's odd appearance, I peer in at what perches amongst the branches and lounges in the shade. Roosting there are all sorts of otherworldly creatures, the kind I do not wish to bump into. Smoldering demons liable to flare up at any time, masturbating Nephilim with colossal appendages, and human spirits with hunted expressions all make their home in or under the tree. As I study the banyan tree's residents, the lyrics to Paul Simon's "Spirit Voices" comes to mind: "We sailed up a river, wide as a sea, and slept on the banks on the leaves of a banyan tree. And all of these spirit voices rule the night." Mental note: do not stray too close to the shrouded banyan.

Here we are in the much-anticipated tropical "paradise" for which we invested ten months of vacation planning. Now, some folks' idea of tropical refers merely to a climate described with words like hot, steamy, stifling. My expectations are more demanding as I desire all five of my senses to be delighted. Now, even I could not ask for more than this beautiful island offers to better fulfill the tropical experience we were promised. Not only does the balmy Jamaican air warm my skin, but the ever-present scents of plumeria, gardenia, and jasmine fancy my nose. Bright fuchsias, purples, and yellows of various plants and flowers join with the beauty of giant bamboo trees. Exotic fruits include the likes of ackee, mammy apple, breadfruit, coolie plum, jackfruit, mangoes (pronounced *MONgoes* by locals), papaya, pineapple, and banana, to name a few—*delectable!* Let's talk about the night sounds. Cicadas and tiny whistling frogs sing in harmony at a pitch and volume comparable to decibels produced by shrill police whistles. They begin their performance by announcing the sunset and carry on until it is the darkest before dawn. Not to worry, as it takes only one restless night to accept it as a soothing singsong lullaby.

What does paradise mean to me? It should include peace, seclusion, and hiding away from dark predatory eyes. Based on my tropical expectations, I naively hoped our island would produce this euphoric paradise condition. I quickly learned this was a fantasy because the opposite is what I have experienced so far. The spiritual atmosphere here is chaotic, loud, wild, and violent. I think that it would border on being painful to live under this pressure constantly, and my heart is baptized with empathy for my island friends.

Besides what I have seen within the banyan, I have also experienced a little island spiritual atmosphere. There's the familiar spirit-bound cat who paid us a visit our first night. After listening to the frogs for two hours, I finally dozed off. For her grand entrance, kitty pounced solidly upon my husband's chest. No, the Villa Dianna is not a feline owner. Yes, one could reason that she was simply conducting her routine prowl. I would have agreed. However, the familiar spirit attached to her by her witch-owner gave away their plot. The second night, Miss Witch herself decided to pay a visit—not in the flesh, mind you. Only her spirit dropped in. With a soothing voice, she whispered, "Don be 'larmed, Sista. We simply observin. *Peace*. No obeah 'pon ya. No harm to ya. No fret, miss. No fret." I later learned that "obeah" means a witchcraft spell. I don't believe either incident was insidiously planned. If I were a witch or a demon, I would check us out. To them, I'm sure we are a curious pair.

I half-expected some spiritual interference on this Caribbean island because I did my research before we ever left American soil. Whenever we visit a foreign country, I desire to know the people, not just the faces tourists want to see. I'm interested in learning what they worship and why. There are publicly worshiped gods, and then there are those no one talks about…, especially to strangers. For instance, many of the early inhabitants of this island were Africans dispersed outside their homeland during the trans-Atlantic slave trade. They practiced Voodoo and worshiped gods that emigrated with them. Worship and sacrifice to these gods spawned numerous demons that do not go away just because the people do. It's not that I'm trying to expose the "secret" gods, but their spirit voices have tormented me night and day since we arrived. Everyone else seems relaxed, happy, and having a lovely time. I am not.

Now, let's add in all the rain. I realize this month is one of two maximum rainfall months, but this constant torrential downpour is a bit ridiculous. I suppose my idea of tropical was a little selfish, as I hadn't factored in the necessary moisture that happens to provide the habitat for plenteous agriculture. Finally, after three days of biblical proportion rain, the weather breaks. The sun shines warmly and creates a terrarium effect, which is fine with me. Being a Midwesterner, I cut my teeth on humid summers.

The six of us are anxious to explore the town, shop at souvenir huts, buy local fruits, and experience some island color. Our friend, Sam, who was born and raised in Jamaica, has talked nonstop about a savory pastry the islanders call patties. A patty is tasty deliciousness baked inside a flaky hand pie crust, much like a turnover or an empanada. They come in three filling choices: beef, chicken, and vegetable. We have anticipated sampling these prizes for three days; today is finally the day!

With our native tour guide behind the wheel, our little group sets out mid-morning in our rented older model six-passenger van. At this point, we are certainly grateful we insisted on one with air conditioning as it's proving to be one sultry day. It is too far to hike to the patty shop from the villa, which is regretful, for driving these washboard roads will loosen up even brand-new cars pretty fast. Down the winding and narrow neighborhood street, past the great banyan tree, bumpity-bump we go. Ugh! My queasy tummy is beginning to wish I had not chosen the back-row seat.

We find the town center and the patty shop within a few minutes. Now, this is quite a busy two-lane, one-way street occupied with drivers who do not necessarily follow any road rules. Unfortunately, we are on the far side of the road, unable to change lanes when we pass the shop. The combination of these circumstances forces us to drive many blocks beyond the patty shop, then unwittingly onto the main highway. Several minutes later, we find a turn-off allowing us to make an about-face back into town. The stress and humor factor has dramatically increased because of some other details: motorists in this country drive on the left side of the road, steering wheels are on the vehicle's right, and all the shifts are flip-flopped from American ones. Therefore, Sam accidentally switches on the windshield wipers when he intends to use the turn signal. This scenario repeats multiple times on our escapade! Born with a "Three Stooges" sense of humor, it is impossible to squelch my belly laughs. I get the feeling that Sam doesn't exactly appreciate my enjoyment.

Eventually, we rediscover the patty shop road, and it appears there is only street parking but no vacancies. Wait! Can it be? There's one spot ahead on the left, directly in front of the shop. *We grab it.*

As soon as the van pulls curbside, a burly guardian angel rushes to my window and leans down to press his face against it. Concentrating his directive at me, he charges, "Don't speak to *that* man," pointing at a scroungy lot attendant leaning against a tiny shack twenty feet away. *"Stay away from him!"* Within seconds, the man makes a beeline for the van to speak with Sam. More animated than before, the angel repeats his warning. "Don't follow him. *Stay put!"* I echo the angel's words to Sam, "Don't speak to that man. Stay here!" Of course, I leave out the part about the angel who just told me this.

"Ev'ryting cool, mon! Ima hook you up. Come dis way…" and the cagey man motions toward a driveway just ahead to our left.

"We shouldn't turn in there!" I shout. Christy, seated beside me, senses my distress, and I fill her in on the angel's warning. Now, she tries to gain Sam's attention, but it's too late. The attendant escorts the van around the side of the building into the driveway. The angel shoots a yearning glance at his helper, another equally menacing angel standing just in front of the van. As quickly as the rear axle crosses the threshold, the attendant is on his cell phone, and another shady man motions us into the lair. We are *trapped* smack-dab in an enclosed lot—buildings in front and on both sides of the "parking lot." Sam tells us to wait in the van and he will return in a few minutes; out he goes. The patty shop is located on the other side of the building to our left, and no sooner does Sam round the corner to the patty shop than a giant pick-up truck pulls in and blocks us.

The angel is back at my window, "Keep your eye on the man in the center of the bench!" Seated on said bench are three men either sleeping or in a drunken stupor. Initially, it isn't clear why I should pay attention to this particular man as he is the teensiest of the three. The man to his left looks older than Methuselah, with snow-white hair going every which way and a booze bottle about to fall from his grasp. The friend on his other side is shirtless and wears urine-stained pants exposing his skinny ribs and bloated belly. None of them appear to be a threat, least of all the little pygmy in the middle.

But just as the angel completes his sentence, the small man cocks his head at a wary angle. Slowly, with staccato movements, he looks up until his yellowish red-speckled eyes focus on me. A kind of vacant expression masks his thin face as if he's in a trance. The longer he fixes his gaze on me, the spirit of a tall man wearing a human skull as a hat begins to materialize about him. Then a hulking giant with a smoking beard situated behind the human spirit man raises its bowed head. Now it is all too clear why the angel told me to keep watch on the pint-sized man—he is obviously a powerful obeah shaman.

With a smileless but amused look on his face, the shaman leisurely moves to his feet. His burnished dreadlocked hair is so long it touches his bandy-legged knees. When he stands, the spirit man and his enormous behemoth stand. Now this ushers in a chaotic brouhaha! A multitude of celestial warriors brandishing swords, rapiers, shields, you name it, suddenly surround my friends and me—backs to us, faces to the obeah man. Since turnabout is fair play, a legion of demons jump from buildings overhead, pop out from beneath anything and everything, and rush in from the street. Empowered by something far superior to him, little guy staggers in our direction. His brutish giant inflates to its grandest height and makes its approach. Urgency is bubbling up in my soul as I fear I will relive something similar to the chaotic spiritual battle scene of my college experience. I describe the present situation to the van passengers in an abbreviated fashion, and my husband decides it's time to retrieve our driver friend from the patty shop. He exits the van. I am relieved to see two massive angels escort him around the corner out of sight.

Now it's just the four of us left in the van…we lock the doors. But I've had about enough of this waiting game. I motion for the scroungy lot attendant to come over to our van, intending to give him some instructions.

"We need to leave. Tell the truck to move right now," I demand in the most Obi-Wan Kanobi way possible.

"No, mon. Mista say he pay me he come back."

"Look. I'll pay you now."

Smiling and demonstratively shaking his head, "Nooo…. Mista muss pay. More time!" He saunters away from the van, obviously dismissing me.

During this exchange, the spiritual stand-off continues outside the van, and a couple of the angels glare wide-eyed at me, imploring me to *hush!* Just as the attendant reaches his corner hut, my husband appears with our driver. Phew! We are all relieved. Sam pays the attendant his due, and miraculously the truck unblocks us. Yummy patties in hand, my husband and our friend climb into the van. Angels, demons, Nephilim, and ancestral human spirits hold their ground, each waiting for the other to back down. Our van backs onto the one-way street, and we drive off casually as if we had just enjoyed a lovely stroll in the park.

* * *

Did we narrowly escape disaster? Did the spirit voices win this one? Napoleon Bonaparte said, "Never interrupt your enemy when he is making a mistake." Who made a mistake? Well, I guess that depends on how you look at it. Did this little band of friends unwittingly tip off the kingdom of darkness to our presence in paradise? Or did our presence in paradise expose the many kinds of spirits that dwell here?

CHAPTER FIFTEEN

Order In Chaos

Order is Heaven's first law.
Alexander Pope

Everything requires order to function properly. Our physical world is specifically ordered, and if one component were misaligned, there would be chaos. For example, galaxies are collections of stars held together by gravity. There are between 100 billion and 200 billion galaxies in the universe, and the Milky Way is the galaxy that contains our solar system, amongst others. There are at least 100 billion planets in the Milky Way and between 200 and 400 billion stars; our sun is just one of them. Our solar system contains nine planets that orbit the sun: Mercury, Venus, Earth, Mars, Jupiter, Saturn, Uranus, Neptune, and Pluto. These planets are held in place by the sun's gravity, and anything that enters our solar system will be sent into orbit around our sun.[1] We see the law of gravity at work on the Earth, also. If an apple falls from a tree, it will hit the ground unless something intercepts it! Gravity always operates and cannot decide one day that it just does not feel like working.

Our souls require order to function properly. Remember, the soul consists of thoughts, emotions, and choices. Our thoughts often dictate to our emotions how to feel about a specific subject then our feelings direct the choices we make concerning it. It goes something like this: Jamaica is a beautiful paradise vacation spot. It has turquoise blue waters, balmy breezes, and a relaxing lifestyle (thoughts). I *love* balmy breezes and warm water. I enjoy being relaxed and carefree (feelings). I will begin planning a vacation to Jamaica right away (choice)! Some of us are more thought directed with our choices, and we lean toward making decisions by weighing the pros and cons of a matter. Psychologists call this *decisional balance:* like a weight scale, one side (the pros) versus the other side (the cons). In this case, our emotions come last in the form of relief, encouragement, sadness, and resolve. How we feel depends on the final decision and how it impacts us.

The human soul and body perform ideally when we develop a healthy spiritual life. Before I explain that statement, let's talk about what I mean by spiritual life, or spirituality, because it is a broad concept with many perspectives. One definition of spirituality is that it's an attitude toward life, making sense of life, relating to others, and seeking unity with the transcendent (higher spiritual power), distinguishing it from religiosity.[2] Another says spirituality is centered on the deepest values and meanings by which people live.[3] It can give higher and deeper meaning to a person's life and inspire them to transcend the ordinary. It is hidden, not overt, yet can manifest energetically.[4]

Spirituality does incorporate elements of religion, but they are not the same thing. Spirituality asks: where do I find meaning, connection, and value? Religion asks: what practices, rites, or rituals should I follow to attain connection and value? The definition this author adopts is: Spirituality is an understanding that people are spiritual creatures with an insatiable need and ability to be united with a higher spiritual power, and that higher power is God. This union transcends our body and soul. In fact, when we are healthy spiritually, our minds, emotions, and bodies benefit.

So many people we meet are controlled by their thoughts. These thoughts control their emotions and negatively affect their physical health. Did you know that 75% to 95% of the illnesses that plague us today directly result from our thought life? In her book *Who Switched Off Your Brain?*, cognitive neuroscientist Dr. Caroline Leaf says, "What we think about affects us physically and emotionally. It's an epidemic of toxic emotions. The average person has over 30,000 thoughts a day. Through an uncontrolled thought life, we create the conditions for illness; we make ourselves sick! Research shows that fear, all on its own, triggers more than 1,400 known physical and chemical responses and activates more than 30 different hormones." This is why people get into the most trouble when focusing on developing their soul or body but neglecting the spirit. Our spirit balances us and allows health and wholeness to flow through our entire being. We are spiritual creatures who need spiritual nurturing. There are multitudes of books and websites that thoroughly educate us on this topic of developing a healthy spiritual life, so I won't go further on it since this chapter is actually on spiritual order. Let's move on.

Like the physical world of human beings, the spirit world also requires structure to function successfully. Yes, even demons depend upon order. Though they are self-promoting narcissists, they understand that the power they need comes from the one ranked above them. What do I mean by that? All spiritual power is delegated from one higher up in authority. Wow! That's a hard concept to accept, but someone has to be in charge. Not everyone can be the leader. We will have a more detailed discussion on the topic of spiritual authority and delegated authority in the next chapter.

For this portion, I will concentrate my explanation of spiritual order on demons, Nephilim, and human spirits. Why am I bringing up spiritual authority and order? Because we see a vivid example of it in the Jamaica story.

The banyan tree.

The banyan tree contained what we like to call the Threefold Cord. The term originates in the Book of Ecclesiastes (4:12) and illustrates a spiritual law, "Though one may be overpowered by another, two can withstand him. And a threefold cord is not quickly broken." The obvious allegory is that three comrades are more victorious if attacked than only two friends. In the same way, I have seen many persistent spiritual strongholds with the combination of Nephilim, demons, and human spirits. Almost nothing will penetrate their fortress. The reason is that demons and Nephilim need willing humans to channel their power through. Once they have them, they're practically unstoppable. All three of these spirit types dwelled in the Banyan. Of course, I didn't stop to inquire about how they came to be there, but they had a spiritual, legal right. They could have owned ancient land rites, meaning people spiritually dedicated the land to them. Maybe the current or previous owner invited them through sacred rituals. Whatever the case, they never leave by their own choice; in reality, they have no choice but to remain bound there. It takes a spiritual cleansing to make them go.

The cat and the witch.

When the cat checked us out on our first night at the Villa Dianna, she wasn't alone. She had a demon, referred to as a familiar spirit, connected to her. The familiar spirit belonged to the witch who appeared the second night to observe us while we slept. Some believe familiars choose the witch, and others believe the witch chooses the spirit. This is merely interesting information but irrelevant. Either way, the spiritual order here is: the witch chose had a familiar spirit (demon) bound to her, and she directed the familiar spirit. Familiars are used for a variety of reasons, all of them to aid the witch. They can be used as an informant to warn her of danger or assist her in accumulating power. We were new to the Villa Dianna, and the witch was curious if we were friendly or adversarial. Would we share our power with her, or would we attempt to take her power from her?

The shaman, the tall man, and the giant.

For this part to make sense, it's necessary for us to review a thumbnail version of Jamaican history. During the Atlantic slave trade, well over 90 percent of all enslaved Africans were imported to the Caribbean and South America. But, the first enslaved people sent to Spanish colonies did not come directly from Africa. They were Christian blacks (ladinos) either African or descendants of Africans, who had been enslaved for a time in Spain. After almost 20 years of this practice, the king of Spain decreed that 4,000 slaves per year should come directly from Africa. Those from the Congo and Angola tribes were not Christianized and brought their ancient religious and magical ways with them. So over time, Jamaica became a profoundly religious society with a wide range of cults, sects, denominations, and movements.[5]

Now, let's focus on the traditions of the Congo as this story relates mainly to them, specifically *Kumina*. Kumina is described as one of the most African religious expressions in Jamaica.[6] Their belief in obeah sorcery embraces several features, including dance, drumming, music, ceremonial spirit possession, animal sacrifice, and the art of healing by using herbs.

The highest-ranking spirits are Oto King Zombi, the Sky God, Obei, and Shango—these spirit beings are believed to dwell in the atmosphere. Earth spirits are the second-highest in rank. They are Cain, Moses, David, Ezekiel, and Shadrach, people who once lived and are mentioned in the Bible's Old Testament. Ancestral spirits are third ranking in authority and also dwell on the Earth. The ancestors were, and continue to be, extremely important to African identity because they form the basis of community identity. Much of the time, a slave owner's horse was considered more valuable than his dehumanized slave. So for 18th-century enslaved black Jamaicans, the community provided the context in which they could be "human."

This is why in Kumina, worship of ancestral spirits is vital. These ancestral spirits are called Zombies; only a person possessed by a Zombi can become a Zombi after death. If a person does not become possessed by Zombies during their lifetime, they will ascend to Oto King Zombi upon death and will not return to Earth. If you are a Kumina practitioner, please don't be offended because I use the term ancestral worship. Merriam-Webster Dictionary defines worship as "reverence, respect, admiration; an act, process, or instance of expressing such veneration by taking part in religious exercises or ritual." So like it or not, you are worshiping ancestral spirits when you sacrifice a goat and use its blood to channel a powerful human spirit Zombi to possess you.

Now that we have the backstory, let's talk about the "pint-sized man, the spirit of a tall man, and his hulking giant." I describe the small man as a powerful obeah shaman. In Kumina, obeahs are believed to be born with special powers passed down from generation to generation, or they've experienced a miraculous conversion that endows them with these powers. Clients seek out the obeah practitioner for spells or charms for various needs, such as help in romantic relationships, physical healing, escape from legal trouble, or even good luck in gambling. Besides these benevolent needs, they cast various curses, hexes, and spells and perform voodoo.

The spirit of a tall man was the ancestral spirit Zombi who possessed the shaman. Ancestral spirits have accumulated a tremendous amount of power throughout the ages. They received their ability via ancestral worship and transference from human body to human body to accomplish their evil goals. Many diasporic traditions practice ancestral worship and transference of spiritual power through transferring human spirits of powerful leaders to their successors.

The hulking giant was a Nephilim bound to the Zombi and, by proxy, the obeah shaman. This experience was a clear example of a spiritual threefold cord: Nephilim, human spirit, and living human. One of those in the threefold cord summoned the various demons that showed up for battle.

CHAPTER SIXTEEN

Kingdom of Darkness Chain of Command

For we do not wrestle against flesh and blood,
but against principalities, against powers,
against the rulers of the darkness of this age,
against spiritual hosts of wickedness in the high places.
Ephesians 6:12

So far, we've discussed the spiritual order of demons, Nephilim, and human spirits. Now, let's broaden our view to include the inhabitants of the kingdom of darkness. This list includes those with no desire to be joined to humans because their responsibility is to influence the spirit world around people. In Chapter 3, I talked about this Class Two type of evil spirits. These beings are located in the second heaven realm and include Satan, principalities, powers, rulers of darkness, and spiritual hosts of wickedness. These are different levels of evil power.

Spirits who seek human connection are fallen angels, therion (that's who Beastie was), Nephilim, unclean spirits, and demons. These entities have different goals and job descriptions that go by many names, such as Jezebel, shame, fear, self-hate, rejection, pride, religious spirit, and that's just the beginning. Each of these strongholds will usually include at least one of each spirit from the list in the first sentence of this paragraph.

Before going there, it's essential to understand the touchy subject of authority. Watchman Nee said, "All things are created through God's authority, and all physical laws of the universe are maintained by His authority. God alone is the authority in all things; all the authorities of the Earth are instituted by God."[1] In understandable language, this means no one and nothing has spiritual or physical authority in or of itself to do anything except what God has already established and delegated. Authority is an awesome thing in the universe—nothing overshadows it. But power and authority are not the same things. A being cannot have power if they do not first have authority. A plainclothes police officer will have difficulty getting people to follow instructions until he whips out his badge. A badge equals authority to wield power.

So every spiritual being mentioned in this book has been delegated their authority by God. That's a lot to take in, especially when these beings make it their mission to torture and destroy us! They do not manufacture their authority; that comes from God. However, their power comes from sin…*our sin*.

Now let's go through the list of spiritual beings in the kingdom of darkness in the order of highest ranking down the ladder.

Satan

I have been asked more times than you might think, "How could a God of love create someone as horrible as the devil?" The short answer is, He didn't. God did not create Satan. God created Lucifer, who was so beautiful that he was known as the day star, the light bearer, giving him the prestigious position of the anointed cherub who covers.[2] Isaiah 14:12-17 tells us that he was the highest-ranking cherub of God's creation.

Then came the moment of rebellion, and five times this beautiful anointed cherub voiced his will in opposition to that of God. Lucifer, the star of the morning, became Satan, the accuser, when he fell to the Earth. Jesus, speaking of this event, said, "I saw Satan fall like lightning from Heaven."[3] Mentioned 15 times in the Old Testament and 32 times in the New Testament, both Hebrew and Greek agree on the meaning of the name: *adversary*. Satan, even though fallen, is still part of the heavenly council but as an accuser. Zechariah 3:1-2 (Jesus Himself is showing Zechariah this vision, not an interpreting angel), "Then he showed me Joshua the high priest standing before the Angel of the Lord, and Satan standing at his right hand to oppose him. And the Lord said to Satan, 'The Lord rebuke you, Satan! The Lord who has chosen Jerusalem rebuke you! Is this not a brand plucked from the fire?'"

In Job 1:6, Satan appears as "the Adversary" to disturb God's kingdom by causing trouble. "Now there was a day when the sons of God came to present themselves before the Lord, and Satan also came among them."

Mark 1:13 says, "And [Jesus] was there in the wilderness forty days, tempted of Satan; and was with the wild beasts (therion), and the angels ministered unto him."

Dr. Guy P. Duffield, in Foundations of Pentecostal Theology, said of Satan: "Though Satan should never be given undue prominence, it is important that the place given him in Scripture be realized. No one other individual, except the Father, the Son, and the Holy Spirit, is afforded so prominent a place in the Bible from its very beginning to its end as the character whom we know as Satan, the Devil. Of no one else are we so minutely informed concerning his origin, his fall, his character and work, his influence, and his ultimate judgment and destiny. We can be deeply thankful for this revelation of him and his host of demons."

Principalities

In Scripture, principalities are always listed first in spiritual authority order. They function second only to Satan himself as the head of spiritual forces marshaled on behalf of spiritual regions of the Earth. Satan gives their orders directly, and they submit to him only. They are mentioned in Scripture as princes of regions (kingdoms) with whom even the Archangel Michael wages war.[4] All of the territory under the principality's authority is considered its kingdom. This kingdom is almost always Earthly continents and sometimes nations. Their borders are usually, though not always, defined by water.

In Greek, the word for principality is *arche* and means a chief of order, time, place, or rank; beginning, ancient.[5] Here are some scripture references to principalities:

Ephesians 1:20-21: [The Father] worked in Christ when He raised Him from the dead and seated Him at His right hand in the heavenly places, far above all principality and power and might and dominion, and every name that is named, not only in this age but also in that which is to come.

Ephesians 3:10: To the intent that now unto the principalities and powers in heavenly [places] might be known by the Church the manifold wisdom of God.

Colossians 1:16: For by Him all things were created that are in heaven and that are on Earth, visible and invisible, whether thrones or dominions or principalities or powers. All things were created through Him and for Him.

Colossians 2:9-10 & 15: For in Him dwells all the fullness of the Godhead bodily; and you are complete in Him, who is the head of all principality and power. Having disarmed principalities and powers, He made a public spectacle of them, triumphing over them in it.

Romans 8:38-39: For I am persuaded that neither death nor life, nor angels nor principalities nor powers, nor things present nor things to come, nor height nor depth, nor any other created thing, shall be able to separate us from the love of God which is in Christ Jesus our Lord.

Powers

Principalities (sometimes referred to as princes) use the powers to "empower" or strengthen the rulers of darkness. The princes have the positional authority—the powers have the might. They have been delegated power by the principalities to do whatever they want, whenever they want to do it.

1 Peter 3:22 mentions powers: [Jesus Christ] has gone into heaven and is at the right hand of God, angels and authorities (*exousia*) and powers (*duna-*

mis) having been made subject to Him. The word authority in Greek is *exousia* and means the authority or right to act, delegated influence, positional authority, and jurisdiction. The word powers in Greek is *dunamis* and means energy, power, might, great force, extraordinary ability, strength, and violence. Exousia is the authority to use dunamis, "force." Here are some scripture references to powers:

Matthew 24:29: Immediately after the tribulation of those days shall the sun be darkened, and the moon shall not give her light, and the stars shall fall from heaven, and the powers (*dunamis*) of the heavens shall be shaken:

Mark 13:25-26: And the stars of heaven shall fall, and the powers (*dunamis*) that are in heaven shall be shaken. And then shall they see the Son of man coming in the clouds with great power and glory.

Luke 21:26: Men's hearts failing them for fear, and for looking after those things which are coming on the Earth: for the powers (*dunamis*) of heaven shall be shaken.

Rulers of Darkness of this World

Directly subject to powers are rulers of darkness of this world or ruling spirits. The Hebrew text for the prince of the kingdom in Daniel 10:13 is *sar malkuwth* meaning "the ruler of rulers of royalty, royal or sovereign power, or dominion. It says, "But the prince of the kingdom of Persia withstood me twenty-one days; and behold, Michael, one of the chief (original, first) princes, came to help me, for I had been left alone there with the kings of Persia (rulers or ruling spirits)."

While on the way to deliver the word of the Lord to Daniel, the messenger was apparently engaged in spiritual warfare somewhere in Persia. This story implies that he was accompanied by other angels when he arrived there, but somewhere along the way, he was "left alone" in the clutches of the ruling spirits. These would be the spiritual "kings" of the cities of Persia, the strongmen. They had already defeated the principalities and powers, and last on his list was to finish off the rulers of darkness. It must have been extremely important that the message was successfully delivered to Daniel because Michael himself was sent to battle on the messenger's behalf. There were probably as many rulers as cities in the Persian Empire at that time.

The New Testament Greek gives an even more explicit picture of a ruler. Ephesians 6:12 says, "For we do not wrestle against flesh and blood, but against principalities, against powers, against the rulers of the darkness of this age, against spiritual hosts of wickedness in the heavenly places." The Greek word for rulers is *kosmokrataor*. It is the Greek word for a military boot camp or training center. *Kosmos* means ordered, arranged, or disciplined. *Kratos* means raw power. So rulers (*kosmokrataor*) are raw power harnessed, arranged, disciplined, then dispatched.[6]

Spiritual Wickedness in High Places

This is a dimension of wickedness that is extreme! The Greek for wickedness is a very foul word. It is *ponēria* and means someone who comes at you with malevolent intent. They don't just want to hurt you; they want to destroy you. They are insidious and violent. These entities are trained, weaponized, then dispatched. John 10:10 says the enemy comes to steal, kill, and destroy. That's probably their mantra as they graduate from Wickedness Academy and are dispatched to their territory: "KILL! STEAL! DESTROY!"

These beings are the spiritual warriors who carry out the bidding of any spiritual entity in authority over them. They put the footwork to the assignments, curses, witchcraft, voodoo, hexes, spells, incantations, and more. They are ranked above only those evil entities who desire to be bound to the human soul.

But, the Apostle Paul describes the location where spiritual wickedness works—high places. There is a spiritual atmosphere above the mountain tops (the Third Heaven) and one below the mountain tops (the Second Heaven). This wickedness conducts warfare in the spirit realm below the mountain-tops—where *we* live.[7]

Paul is speaking by divine revelation in Ephesians 6:12. He looked into the spirit realm and saw how Satan's kingdom is aligned militarily. I am genuinely thankful that Paul not only saw into the spirit realm but that God gave him the revelation to understand what he saw, and he wrote it down. Because he did, 2000 years later, we have a window into understanding what we see!

Now we come to spirits that can be bound to humans. These are listed in rank order: fallen angels, therion, Nephilim, unclean spirits, and demons. Because I have already described everything except the therion, I will do so here.

Therion

Therion is the Greek word for *beast*—the wild, brutal, savage, and ferocious kind. Beastie was this type of spirit, specifically a mega therion. Mega therion is the highest-ranking of therion. Here are some Bible verses that mention therion:

Mark 1:13: And He was there in the wilderness forty days, tempted by Satan, and was with the wild beasts; and the angels ministered to Him.

1 Corinthians 15:32: If, in the manner of men, I have fought with beasts at Ephesus, what advantage is it to me? If the dead do not rise, "Let us eat and drink, for tomorrow we die!"

Revelation 6:8: So I looked, and behold, a pale horse. And the name of him who sat on it was Death, and Hades followed with him. And power was given to them over a fourth of the Earth, to kill with sword, with hunger, with death, and by the beasts of the Earth.

If you want to research therion on your own, find a good Bible concordance and search for beast in the New Testament. You'll find it's used 46 times, and not every time is referring to a spirit. Acts 28:5 is just one case where therion is an actual venomous snake. But almost every verse using therion in the Book of Revelation refers to *The* Beast at the end of days, which we know is a powerful spirit controlled by Satan. For example, Revelation 11:7 says, "When they finish their testimony, the beast that ascends out of the bottomless pit will make war against them, overcome them, and kill them." Also, Revelation 13:1 and 4, "Then I stood on the sand of the sea. And I saw a beast rising up out of the sea, having seven heads and ten horns, and on his horns ten crowns, and on his heads a blasphemous name. So they worshiped the dragon who gave authority to the beast; and they worshiped the beast, saying, "Who is like the beast? Who is able to make war with him?"

Timothy and I have ministered to many ex-Satanists needing freedom from therions. There are several kinds, and each has an extensive job description, but I'm not going to go into detail about them now. Let's just say they are immensely evil, ruthless, and violent. Their endgame is complete possession of the human host.

PART 6

To Be Absent From the Body

CHAPTER SEVENTEEN

A Celebration of Death

Talk about dull! This Emergency Room is as exciting as watching paint dry. It's nothing like Rampart General Hospital in that '70s television series, *Emergency!* No Nurse Dixies scurrying about treating each person with individual care and immediate attention. Only poor souls waiting many hours for medical treatment.

Where I live, the term Emergency Room has become a kind of misnomer. What I mean by where I live is a cramped, overflowing West Coast city affectionately known as "The City of Angels"—another misnomer. In the last decade, scores of hospitals have shut down their emergency rooms due to high operating costs and lack of funding. So, when one happens upon a hospital with the nearly extinct Emergency Room in commission, it is plagued with overcrowding and long waits.

The first thing folks learn once they arrive at the Emergency Room is that what they believe qualifies as an "emergency" does not in any way guarantee they will be treated as if they have one. There is the man in the corner who has vomited blood all over the chair and floor. Another man leans against a wall looking ghastly gray, holding a heavily blood-soaked bandaged hand above his head. The young mother clutching a lethargic toddler bundled with baby blankets, though it's 90 degrees outside. These cases I would personally diagnose these as emergencies. Of course, I am not a doctor, nor am I trained medically in any way. I'm only here to visit my friend, who has already been taken behind the locked and guarded door to be treated for his medical emergency.

I inquire about Joshua with the nurse guard in the booth protected by the bulletproof glass window. At her request, I produce my photo identification card, I'm scanned for weapons, and she buzzes me in through the solid metal door. This whole process inspires my prohibitive conscience to make me feel guilty about some lethal secret, especially as the door latches behind me. This is the most exciting thing that has happened since I arrived!

On the other side, I walk past eight occupied hospital beds immersed in antiseptic cologne before I find Joshua at the end, tucked away in a corner with a white curtain pulled halfway around him. To his right is an empty bed—the only one in the ER. As I look around, it still seems to me that there should be more action here. I sit in a metal chair next to Joshua's bed and ask how he's feeling. He's much better, but he's been here for six hours now, and the potent pain meds have kicked in. The doctors are running more tests to get to the bottom of his symptoms. At least they've ruled out cancer—maybe it's a kind of infection. They're just not sure. I am relieved, and we continue chitchatting.

Eventually, I notice the bloated fiftyish man on the other side of the empty bed next to Joshua. He is unconscious and motionless. There is a quality in his face, some grinning sadness suggesting a clown minus makeup. A few minutes later, he becomes restless and begins to whimper. I ask Josh if he knows why the man is here. Apparently, paramedics accompanied by two police officers wheeled him in this morning. He overheard bits of their conversation that included words such as "overdose," "not the first time," and "heroin." Josh says his neighbor pleaded several times with God to take his life.

I feel sorry for the mournful man. I can see his monitors, his exposed feet and legs, then a white sheet loosely covering the rest of his nakedness. He's moaning now, but no one seems to notice him as there is a flurry of activity surrounding a bed at the other end of the room where most of the nurses have rushed. I turn my attention back to Joshua.

Our conversation moves to sports and other nonessential topics for a few moments. Because curiosity gets the best of me, I check over my shoulder to see how the person at the other end of the room with the nurse hive is progressing. That's when I notice our Heroin-overdosed neighbor's feet are *blue*. A swift motion catches my peripheral attention, and I snap my head to see what activity is taking place in the hallway. Oh, no! The swift motion is the spirit of the man with the blue feet, who has left his body, now peering in from the hallway. Concurrently, shrill tones are sounding from his medical monitors because now his body is gurgling and convulsing. It seems like many moments pass before a nurse finally arrives, yelling, "Code Blue! Code Blue!" drawing at least two more nurses and one doctor to his side.

I turn my attention back to the man's spirit in the hallway, where two cheerful angel escorts have appeared on either side of him. "What are you doing out there? *Get back in here!*" I mouth to him, motioning with my hands toward his body. Shrugging his shoulders, he flashes his clown-like grin at me. Now he's bouncing and trouncing in place, smiling from ear to ear like a giddy schoolboy. Rather than following my advice, he takes hold of the hands of the angelic being to his left and dances around the hallway, skipping and turning to silent music. I feel powerless to convince him to rejoin his body. It is a peculiar, desperate feeling to communicate with a person who desires to die more than to live.

The man occasionally pauses his celebratory jig to check in on the progress of the medical staff attending to his body. If I were in his position, I would begin to feel great discouragement because it looks like the team has virtually exhausted every one of their resuscitation options. On the contrary, the telltale ear-piercing tone produced by his flat-lined heart monitor only brings shrieks of laughter from him. "Whoo hoo!" and "Let's go!" are the delightful squeals coming from the hallway. Sadness and sorrow left behind, the man and his joyful entourage triumphantly skip down the hallway out of sight.

Emily Dickenson wrote, "Hope is the thing with feathers that perches in the soul and sings the tune without the words and never stops at all...." Some folks hope in things other folks fear. My new friend hoped in death, for it was his only escape from his addiction prison. So, courtesy of the heroin captor who bound him in this life, he was finally free to fly away.

CHAPTER EIGHTEEN

A Solitary Act

*"No, no, no life! Why should a dog, a horse, a rat,
have life, and thou [Cordelia] no breath at all?
Thou'lt come no more, never, never, never, never, never."*
Lear, King of Britain
"King Lear," Act V, William Shakespeare

It's difficult to talk a person out of dying when they have set their mind to it. Sometimes no amount of coaxing will convince them to live—not even to live for us. When Mr. Edward Magorium was about to depart this life, he said, "When King Lear dies in Act V, do you know what Shakespeare has written? He's written, 'He dies.' That's all—nothing more. No fanfare, no metaphor, no brilliant final words. The culmination of the most influential work of dramatic literature is, 'He dies.' It takes Shakespeare, a genius, to come up with 'He dies.' And yet, every time I read those two words, I find myself overwhelmed with dysphoria. And I know it's only natural to be sad, not because of the words 'He dies,' but because of the life we saw prior to the words. I've lived all five of my acts...and I am not asking you to be happy that I must go. I'm only asking that you turn the page, continue reading, and let the next story begin. And if anyone asks what became of me, you relate my life in all its wonder and end it with a simple and modest 'He died.'"[1]

To the living, death seems final and lonely. It used to pain me to think of someone alone when they died. At the very least, someone should hold their hand or touch their arm as they pass. But this was before I was present with a dying person and watched what took place in the spiritual realm around them at the end. Their solitary act no longer anguishes me because I know they are far from being alone. Maybe you've witnessed it, too.

I wish I could say that I can see where our spirits ultimately go after our bodies die. I cannot. I have talked to people who tasted death and were revived. Each story is similar to what they saw and experienced.

I have been present with several people when they died. I watched a man die lying on his living room floor. I watched a woman die on the floor of a craft store. I watched another man die in his crumpled car after he was fatally wounded in a four-car pileup on the freeway. Of course, I watched the man die in his hospital bed in this story.

These four experiences do not make me an expert on death and dying. However, I did observe two things that were consistent with each experience. The first is that the death of the body is not the end of life because the spirit lives on. The second is that death is not a lonely experience. If they are willing to go, each person has two angels to escort them from this physical existence.

In chapter seven, I addressed why some human spirits do not move on to the afterlife when their bodies die. The pertinent question is, why do most people move on to the afterlife when their bodies die? The first reason is that if they are born again, then their spirits are alive, and they will go directly to the Third Heaven to be in the presence of God.[2] The second reason they move on is that they have not broken a moral law (such as revenge, murder, obsession, hatred, or violence) binding their spirit to someone or someplace. They are at peace with death and ready to pass on.

I understand now that the only sadness and loneliness in death remains with the living who have lost the one they love. Harriet Beecher Stowe said, "The bitterest tears shed over graves are for words left unsaid and deeds left undone."

Other types of out-of-body experiences.

Physical death is not the only way for the spirit to leave the body. There is a method called out-of-body experience, where a person's spirit seems to float outside their living body. This experience is common in near-death situations but occurs at other times, also. Some terms used interchangeably to refer to this practice are astral projection, remote viewing, or lucid dreaming. There are several methods used to achieve an out-of-body experience. However, I am not going to discuss them here. Some people practice out-of-body experiences because they believe they will gain a new perspective on life and self; others to escape present circumstances.

Sometimes when someone has an out-of-body experience, they can see themselves still attached to their physical body by an energy connection that looks like a silver cord, somewhat like an umbilical cord. They believe that as long as this cord is attached, they are entirely safe and able to return to their body whenever they choose. This cord functions similarly to the soul tie we discussed in chapter eleven.

On a warm night the summer after the dorm room fiasco, Holly and I were about to leave for the dance club when my friend, Curt, called to invite us to a house party. We thought, why not? We'll stop by the party to jump-start our night of shenanigans. So, we do just that. Not only is there a generous supply of weed floating around, but someone planned ahead and filled a watermelon with Everclear. What a fantastic idea! After about an hour, we start out the door to get on with the night of fun. The house party host stopped us at the front door because he said he had something special for me.

"What is it?" I ask, always game for something different. He takes a tiny pill out of his pocket and hands it to me. "If you eat half of this, you'll feel like you drank a six-pack," he says. This sounds like a great plan to me so I take it. Yes, the whole thing. Why? I suppose after smoking weed for an hour and eating my weight in Everclear-spiked watermelon, my judgment wasn't too sharp. Off we go!

Fast forward to about an hour later of drinking cocktails and dancing at the club, I was beginning to feel pretty out of it. I became seriously worried when I leaned against a wall talking to Curt, and slid to the floor. He was extremely alarmed and had to carry me to Holly's car. The last thing I remember is hanging my head out the passenger seat window as Curt drove us to his house. He told me later that I was completely unconscious, so he carried me in and laid me on the couch.

When I finally woke up, the clock on the living room wall said 2:15 am. *Holy crap! I'm in so much trouble!* I was supposed to be home by midnight. I go to the back door to see if Holly's car is still there, but it's not. I'm guessing she's at home because her curfew is also at midnight. Maybe I could sneak in my house and no one would know I wasn't home at midnight. That was wishful thinking, as there are no cars in the driveway, which is a little confusing. How am I going to get home?

I go back into the house and decide to call Holly. Maybe she could pick me up and take me to her house. I could just tell my parents I decided to spend the night with her. I'm having trouble getting the buttons on the phone to work so I give up on that plan. I glance into the bedroom and see that Curt is asleep, lying crosswise on the bed. I try to wake him, but no luck. I'm beginning to feel desperate and very alone.

As I turn around to leave the bedroom, I see someone else asleep in the living room. Maybe I can wake her! But, as I approach the couch, I realize the girl lying on it is *me!* Now what?! This is definitely not good that my body is there and my spirit is here! Before I begin to panic, I start to pray. And the simple thought came to me, "*Sit down on your body and you will enter it.*" Apparently, it worked, because 4 hours later, I was awakened by Curt's hand hovering over my nose, checking for breath.

During this out-of-body experience, I didn't see my silver cord attached to my body. I also didn't see any angel escorts, which is a very good thing! One would think that Roofie/alcohol overdose would've been my "Come to Jesus" moment. It wasn't. But I'm thankful it didn't cause Him to stop pursuing me. Satanists also practice out-of-body travel, but their reasons are far from recreational. The highly skilled can leave their body and travel undetected to people and places to curse them. I have a dramatic experience with just such a Satanist.

Initially, the interruption of sound awakened me. A small fan I use every night to provide me enough white noise to drown out the demonic clatter sits bedside, my husband Timothy situated between. I had been asleep for about two hours when something, or someone, passed between the fan and the bed. I checked the clock—1:03 am.

I bolted up and turned toward the fan. Much to my surprise (and discomfort), I saw an African man standing beside the bed, *leaning over my husband.* He wore a long-sleeved white and gold native shirt with a small ceremonial cap on his head and waved a pocket watch in a circular motion over my husband. He concentrated so intently on his work that he didn't notice me, even though I sat up and stared right at him. Once I realized I was looking at a human spirit and not a physical intruder, I said to him, "What are you doing here?" Startled, he jumped back, stared at me with wide eyes, then quickly turned and ran. I quietly leaned on one elbow for a few moments, watching to be sure he didn't return, then turned over and went back to sleep.

The next day was busy, and I didn't give the nighttime visitor a second thought. We were preparing to travel to Nigeria in a few weeks, and my days were packed with details. That night I fell into bed and looked forward to a good night's rest. About an hour and a half later (the clock again read 1:03 am), I was awakened as something heavy crawled onto the foot of the bed. I whirled around and sat face to face with the same African man who had appeared the night before. This time, he held two gold coins between his left-hand fingers and waved them in a circular motion above our bodies.

"What do you think you're doing?" I snapped at him. A reenactment of the night before followed as he retreated through the bedroom door. This time I made a mental note to remember to share these two experiences with my husband the next day.

A few years before this, an ex-Satanist friend shared many stories about how they used to practice what the African man was doing in our bedroom. This friend also explained how simple it is to prevent a person from astral projecting into our home whenever they pleased. It is common practice amongst Satanists to use spiritual laws of the Christian Bible as the driving force behind their magic. One law Satanists use to control their enemies when they are astral projecting is Ecclesiastes 12:6-7. It says, "Remember your Creator before the silver cord is *loosed*...then the dust (the body) will return to the Earth as it was, and the spirit will return to God who gave it." Remembering our friend's advice, it's the spiritual law Timothy and I also used.

On the third night, we quoted Ecclesiastes 12:6-7 and said that as soon as the African man entered our bedroom, his silver cord connecting him to his body would be loosed (severed), and his spirit would return to God. I'll admit that it was pretty difficult for me to fall asleep that night. It is an uncanny feeling to anticipate that in a couple of hours, a stranger might leave his body and invade our home with the express purpose of causing us spiritual harm. I tried not to think about it and eventually fell asleep.

This time (again, 1:03 am), I was awakened when a bright flash of light, much like lightning, filled our room. I sat up just in time to see the African man begin to crawl onto our bed. Almost simultaneously, I noticed two large angels on either side of the man. Like a deer caught in headlights, he looked at me and quickly turned his head to glance behind him. As if someone had turned on a giant vacuum, he was sucked backward from the room! This time I woke my husband to report what had happened. We were both immensely relieved.

Weeks later, on our Nigeria trip, we learned that Juju priests (powerful local witch doctors) leave their bodies to curse people in their homes. We heard reports that they have seriously injured and even killed some people during these out-of-body experiences. Thankfully, our Juju priest didn't get that far.

PART 7

Freedom From the Tormentors

As I have already expressed,
this book is about my personal journey.
I believe it would border on negligence if I didn't share
the deliverance and inner healing pathway
that got me to where I am today.
This final part of the book begins with my freedom from the beast.
I will also give you precise methods and prayers
so you can be freed from your tormentors.

CHAPTER NINETEEN

Who Shall Separate Us?

It's eerily quiet. No sight nor sound of the beast for at least five days. Either he's in hiding, which would be a first, or he's chosen to leave me for good. The latter is impossible since he's bound to me through hundreds of generations of legal rights. I don't know if I should relax in his truancy or be on guard. Experience tells me this so-called state of peace is not of God; it is simply the absence of war. I have learned not to rest in it. There's no resting, anyway. Until the beast is permanently cast out, there's no predicting his next stranglehold.

After 31 years of ongoing torment, May 25th, 1995, has arrived. I make my way to the church a few minutes early for my 1:00 pm appointment and take a seat in the waiting area of the Pastoral Care Office. Whew! I made it here safe and sound—no Beastie.

"Denise? Denise?" It's a familiar woman's voice, but not my mother's. She sounds so far away. "Denise?" Why does she continue repeating my name? It's a bit annoying! Like when you're having a good nap and someone interrupts it.

The thing is, I know I am not asleep, but I am not present either. It's not the first time they have dragged me down into this neutral place of my soul. It's as if one minute you're floating in a calm body of water, and the next, something takes hold of your ankles and pulls you under. Only there is no welcoming escape of death here. You are simply at their mercy in a hellish holding pattern within their chambers.

There's that voice again. Oh! It's Helen. "Denise, Pastor Timothy is ready for you." Ugh. Well, there is no use being embarrassed about it. I'm sure it's not the strangest thing Helen has experienced this week. She's been Pastor Timothy's secretary for many years and has seen just about everything imaginable.

My legs feel weak, but I will them to carry me into the office. Pastor Timothy greets me, "Hello, Denise. Are you ready to defeat the beast today?" All I hear in my head is, "*F#@k you, a**hole!*" And there he is. I guess Beastie did not choose to leave me for good. My, my, my, how it hates Pastor Timothy! By now, we've learned that this beast is a therion[1] and doesn't take too kindly to being challenged.

"Yes. I'm ready," I confirm with certainty. I sit down in a chair opposite his desk.

"Let's begin. In Jesus' name, I cover this room with the blood of Jesus. I sever every tie to the principalities, powers of the air, rulers of darkness, and spiritual hosts of wickedness in heavenly places.[2] I sever all ties known and unknown between the ruler of darkness over Van Nuys, California, and this beast...." I'm sure he prayed some other powerful things, but it began to feel as if Pastor Timothy droned on and on.

Somewhere in the middle of his prayer, I had been pulled under again, and the beast was speaking through me with pure hatred and fury. "Shut your *f#@$ing* mouth, you pathetic mortal. Who do you think you are? You know she's mine. She was passed on to me generations and generations ago, long before you could pee standing up."

"Well, hello there, beast. You do want to spend some time with me! It's your last day." Though he comes across as if he's sparring with them, Pastor Timothy knows we gain position in the battle when we can provoke evil spirits to lose their composure. Let's just say he's really good at it!

Pastor Timothy continues, "Beast, I bind you. Be still and go down. Denise, come back up. Come back. You're safe." Woosh! I'm back and present. One might wonder why Pastor Timothy would bind the beast and command it to go down. I mean, isn't it the goal to get him up and out? Yes, it is the *final* goal, but not quite yet. At this point in the battle, removing all spiritual legal rights the beast has that keep him bound to me is critically important. Otherwise, we will be here fighting until tomorrow, and that's a long, exhausting battle. It takes more than sheer spiritual authority and willpower to cast out evil spirits. Even Jesus spent time talking to the epileptic boy's father to find out what legal rights the demon had to torment him.[3]

"Are you ready to pray?" he asks.

"Yes. I'm ready to cast out the beast." My resolve is sure, but my body is trembling, and my stomach feels queasy.

"Okay, Denise. Repeat this prayer after me: Father, I repent for every known and unknown sin my ancestors or I have committed, giving the beast a legal right to be bound to me." Thankfully, Pastor Timothy broke this prayer up into small chunks so I could get the words out. The beast fought the whole while to hang on to any shred of control he had. But I fought harder.

We continue, "I renounce the beast. I remove his rights and ability to stay bound to me." Though the beast hated the repenting part, he utterly abhorred the renouncing part! When we repent, we speak to God. We confess the sin or wrongdoing to Him with a heart attitude to turn away from it and never do it again. But when we renounce, we speak directly to the hellish spirit, removing its legal right and control over us.

I barely get the word "renounce" out of my mouth, and the beast furiously shoves me aside. "Who the hell do you think you are, Preacher? I've had enough of you. We're leaving."

"Great! That was the plan. So leave, in Jesus' Name," Pastor Timothy declares.

"That's not what I meant, and you know it. You think you're so smart sitting behind your little desk in your black suit and outdated tie. All I have to do is command a couple of my minions to attack you, and you're dead."

"Go ahead, Beastie. If you could kill me, I'd already be dead."

Silence.

"Whatever. Then I'll kill her. She's completely worthless to me now. She's a total failure, a complete disappointment. She will never amount to anything."

"Go ahead and kill her. If you could do it, she'd be dead by now."

"Aha! Exactly what I've been telling her all along. You don't care about her. You could care less if she lives or dies. All you care about is if you make it to your tee time at 4:30. So why don't you stop dragging this *s#*!* out and quit while you're ahead."

I hear all of this as clearly as if I'm sitting in the corner of the room, eavesdropping on someone's conversation about me. I understand the beast wants to intimidate me and provoke Pastor Timothy. He also wants to divide us by saying Pastor Timothy doesn't care about me. If I believe the beast, then I stop trusting Pastor Timothy. If I stop trusting him, then I will be in disunity with him. It is critically important that we are in agreement with each other because of the spiritual law: when two agree about what they ask for, it will be done for them by Father God.[4]

Hey Beastie—*bring it!* Now it's my turn to shove him aside. "Let's keep praying, Pastor Timothy!"

"Okay! Continue to repeat after me: Father God, I break all soul ties, all spirit ties, all demonic ties, every Nephilim tie, all unclean spirit ties, all emotional ties, and all ties to every broken part of my soul that the beast holds on to. I flood every broken part with living water and cleanse each one from every touch and all debris from the beast. I flood them with the precious blood of Jesus, which brings healing to them. Jesus, heal their wounds right now."

By the time I got to the first "break," I could not speak, but my spirit mind was in complete agreement with the entire prayer.[5]

"Okay, okay. Hold your horses, Preacher. Let's talk about this. I have a lot of people in here that you might be interested in saving. After all, aren't you in the business of saving souls?" Oh, how quickly the beast transitioned from boasting to bargaining. He must be feeling the pressure now.

"Sure. Go ahead and release them. Father, I repeat the words of my Savior when he hung on the cross: into Your hands, I commit these spirits. I break all soul ties and spirit ties between the beast and the unclean spirits. Leave now." Pastor Timothy commanded.

Suddenly, there is a mass exodus of terrified, crying, and some overjoyed people fleeing for their lives. I exhale and cough for several minutes as these poor souls are, at long last, received into the loving arms of Jesus. Many, many angels come and go as they escort them from this planet to their final resting place. I can only imagine how long some of them have been trapped here.

As highly intelligent as the beast is, I don't think it occurs to him that we will continue to pursue him even after he has thrown these spirits under the bus. But my determination has not wavered in the least. In fact, I was more tenacious now than in the beginning. I was finally winning!

"Father," Pastor Timothy prayed, "thank You for removing these unclean spirits. Now, in Jesus' name, I command the beast to leave my sister! Beast, be gone! Leave her. I take authority over you, and according to 1 John 5:8, I flood your inner chambers with the Three Witnesses on Earth—the water, the blood, and the Holy Spirit."

"What do you think you're doing? We had a deal!"

"No, we did not have a deal. I don't negotiate with puny demons such as you. Now leave my sister."

The next thing I know, I am heaved into the air and thrown onto the floor. I hear growling, gnashing, and spitting coming from somewhere. I can only conclude that it is coming from the beast. He is writhing around, and it feels like a large foot has been thrust into his back, pinning him to the carpet. Of course, everything happening to the beast simultaneously happens to my body since he's inside me. Pastor Timothy continues battling.

"Please stop tormenting me," the beast pathetically begs. Well, that's the first time I have EVER heard him say please! "I promise I won't bother her again. I'll retreat to my inner chambers and stay put, never to be seen again."

"Beast, you have a problem with short-term memory. I flooded your inner chambers with the Three Witnesses about 20 minutes ago. You can't return."

Silence. Except for the labored wheezing, it seems like he is gone.

"Beast, your time is up. You've never been cast out before, have you? All you have ever done is transfer from person to person. Well, this will be an exciting new experience for you. You're about to be cast out by a *girl!*"

Again, silence. I can sense the beast is thinking and trying to come up with some shred of legal right or scheme to outwit Pastor Timothy. Then, on the verge of tears, the beast whispers, "I purchased her. Thousands of people bled and died so I could have her as my own. If you cast me out, you desecrate their sacrifice."

As cool as can be, Pastor Timothy said, "Beast, show me your receipt. You say you purchased Denise? Then show me your receipt." Silence. "You don't have one because Jesus Christ purchased your ownership papers. He purchased every handwriting of requirement against her and nailed it to His cross.[6] He bought and paid for her redemption. He bled. He died. But the difference is, He lives! He holds her receipt. You hold nothing."

And just like that, Jesus is standing beside my limp body lying facedown on the carpet. My Jesus has come for me! How do I know it's Him and not just an angel? I know the feeling of His presence. The sound of His voice is familiar to me. I see the look of love in His eyes as He leans down to me, holds out His hand, and says, "I'm here. I came to rescue you today. Take my hand and watch this."

Instantly, I step out of my body, grasp my savior's hand, and stand beside Him. I can hear Pastor Timothy command the beast to leave, and I can see my body convulsing under the agony of the beast. I wonder if my body will survive! Will I ever hold my babies or see my parents again in this life? Even though these are simply thoughts and I do not speak the words, Jesus turns to me and says, "My love, even if your body dies, I will raise it up again. Do you trust Me?" I say, "Yes, Lord! With all that I am, I trust You." And just like that, the beast is gone. In a blink of an eye, my spirit is instantly back in my body, and Jesus is gone. I begin weeping with joy and gratitude.

Truly, who shall separate us from the love of Christ? Shall trouble or hardship or persecution or famine or nakedness or danger or sword? No, in all these things we are more than conquerors through Him who loves us. For I am convinced that neither death nor life, neither angels nor demons, neither the present nor the future, nor any powers, neither height nor depth, nor anything else in all creation, will be able to separate us from the love of God that is in Christ Jesus our Lord.[7] It is this immeasurable love, this vast and deep love, that separates us from the tormentors.

CHAPTER TWENTY

Weapons of Warfare

> *"If you know the enemy and know yourself,*
> *you need not fear the result of a hundred battles.*
> *If you know yourself but not the enemy,*
> *for every victory gained you will also suffer a defeat.*
> *If you know neither the enemy nor yourself,*
> *you will succumb in every battle."*
> Sun Tzu, The Art of War

The first step in casting out every kind of spirit in Satan's kingdom is to know our enemies' strengths, weaknesses, and strategies. In the previous six parts of this book, I describe what I understand about these inhabitants and how they use humans to accomplish their selfish goals. I don't pretend to know *everything* about them, only what I have experienced so far. I hope you know more about your enemy today than when you started reading this book.

But as necessary as it is to know our enemy, we need to know our weapons of warfare. At the onset of the battle against Beastie, Pastor Timothy led me through a specific prayer. The three points to it are repent, renounce, and break. But what is the point of this, and why is it necessary? I'm delighted you asked!

Prayer: Repent, Renounce, Break

The Apostle Paul instructed his mentee Timothy: "In meekness instruct those that oppose themselves; if God will lead them to repentance and acknowledge the truth."[1] In other words, those who oppose themselves must see the truth and then repent. Oppose themselves? This is when we self-sabotage and get in our own way. Someone said, "I'm only attracted to the bad boys. The nice ones are too boring for me." Even though nearly all of her relationships ended in abuse and heartache, she just didn't see how she opposed herself by pursuing the "bad" ones. Once we understand how we oppose ourselves, then we repent. The best way to see how we oppose ourselves is to increase our knowledge of what the Word of God says about our behavior or beliefs.

Repent

To turn away from the act, the sin, with the intent never to do it again. When we repent, we ask God for forgiveness and remission of sin.

Renounce

This is a legal term and means to remove its legal right to stay. When we renounce, we're speaking to the spirit we want freedom from, and we're expressing our will to be separated from it.

Break

This part is pretty self-explanatory. We break the soul tie, the tie to the spirit, the power of the spirit, the curse, etc. Whatever the specific prayer is intended to rid ourselves of is what we break.[2]

As a final thought, we usually spend more time on the repent and renounce parts than on the break part. This is because we want to thoroughly remove every legal right that we can so that the breaking can happen.

The Three Witnesses

This brings us to one of my favorite subjects, the Three Witnesses. They are so amazing! But what are they? Technically there are five witnesses, but we will focus on the three that are on Earth. This makes more sense when we read 1 John 5:7, "For there are three that bear witness in Heaven: the Father, the Word (Christ), and the Holy Spirit; and these three are one." Raise your hand if that's an easy statement to agree on. Okay, next verse, "And there are three that bear witness on Earth: the Spirit, the water, and the blood; and these three agree as one." Seems straightforward. But how do water and blood agree with the Spirit? Aren't they simply inanimate matter? This verse sounds like they can make a choice. Before we get there, let's begin by defining what a witness is.

- One who gives evidence.
- One who testifies in a cause or before a judicial tribunal.
- One asked to be present at a transaction so as to be able to testify to its having taken place.
- One who has personal knowledge of something.[3]

The New Testament Greek word for witness is *martyria*, and this is where we get our English word martyr. This definition is a bit more serious than presenting evidence and personal knowledge. It refers to those who had been eye-witnesses and ear-witnesses of the extraordinary sayings, works, and sufferings of Jesus and were willing to die for their testimony. And Apostle John says water and blood are martyrs for Jesus—witnesses. But it is the Holy Spirit who makes them so.

The Witness of the Spirit

Holy Spirit is not an "it" or a thing—He is a real person. He doesn't seek to be mysterious, but He is the most mysterious of the Trinity. We can read in the Word about the Father, and we can read about the Son, but Jesus tells us that when the Spirit comes, "He will guide you into all truth. He will not speak on his own authority but will speak whatever he hears and will tell you what is to come. He will glorify me because He will receive from me what is mine and will tell it to you."[4]

God's love has been poured out into our hearts *through* the Holy Spirit, who is a gift to us.[5] He convicts every person of sin and teaches, equips, and empowers Christ followers, but that's not all He does. Before Jesus came, the people were led by the law (which included the Ten Commandments). In and of itself, the law was good for the purpose God intended it to accomplish, which was to make them conscious of what was sinful and create a sense of guilt over it. Although it showed the people what was wrong with them, it did nothing to help them change or improve. Now that the law has been empowered by grace and truth, Jesus and our trust in Him can change us. The Holy Spirit, also called the Spirit of Grace, is the administrator of that transformation. Even with the best intentions to improve our behavior through hard work and daily effort, we need the Holy Spirit's help.

Just as Father God and Jesus the Son are eternal, the Holy Spirit is also eternal. We might think that eternal means something that always continues from this point forward and has no end. But this explanation tells us only what eternal is not and says nothing about its nature or being. Andrew Murray said, "Everything that exists in time has a beginning and is affected by the law of increase and decrease, of becoming and decaying. What is eternal has no beginning and knows no change or weakening because it has a life independent of time. In what is eternal, no past has disappeared and is lost, and no future is not yet possessed. It is always an endless present in which an imperishable life works ceaselessly every moment."[6]

The workings of the eternal Holy Spirit are invisible and gentle, and within them, as I have already stated, He never tells us about Himself. So the symbols of the Holy Spirit become essential to our understanding of what He's like, not only in an objective way of analyzing truth but also in the subjective way that He comes to penetrate our lives—ways in which the reality of the invisible penetrates the visible. For example, when we talk about the Holy Spirit as rain, the purpose isn't to think, "Oh, the Holy Spirit is like rain." The purpose is to get wet.

Holy Spirit desires to move into our realm in each of the following seven ways. Just as the Holy Spirit manifested for a moment in a dove and lighted upon Jesus when He came up from the baptismal water, He wants to penetrate you and me with the glory of the invisible God that becomes visible in us—to flood His life into ours that we might then overflow it to others.

The Holy Spirit Comes as Rain.

Rain has a dual implication. First, as refreshing where there has been dryness and barrenness.[7] Second, as restoration where there has been loss.[8] The "pouring out" Apostle Peter refers to at Pentecost[9] is not an abstract use of the word; it has to do with the "latter rain" that brought about the harvest. The Lord is saying that He will send rain to fields [people] that are totally barren as a promise of hope.

Needing to be refreshed doesn't mean that I've sinned. When the lawn endures a hot day, it dries up and needs the refreshing of rain. The Holy Spirit, coming as rain, comes to bring refreshing and restoration.

The Holy Spirit Comes as Rivers.

Rivers are channels or conduits to places where the refreshing of water is needed. John pinpoints that the work of the Spirit as "rivers of living water" was to become available after Jesus' ascension.[10] The Lord wants people to get in touch with who He is, and that takes people who will let the rivers of living water be awakened in them and then gush out of their lives. So the Holy Spirit is manifest in rivers.

The Holy Spirit Comes as Wind.

The Holy Spirit, coming as wind, describes His power and His guidance. When Jesus tells Nicodemus about the new birth experience,[11] He tells him that it is not like a real birth where you can see the baby is born and check the clock for its arrival time. The work of the Spirit breathes into a life, and something transpires that people cannot recognize. There's a dynamism but also a gentleness, like the wisp of a breeze. You can't necessarily see where it came from or where it goes, but all of us can attest to times when God has come and dealt with us, and no human being knew how it happened.

At Pentecost,[12] it wasn't a wind that blew in; it was the *sound* of a rushing wind—like a hurricane. That sound, not the sound of the people speaking in tongues, is what drew the crowd in. The Holy Spirit as sovereign God is dynamic, irresistible, and unstoppable.

The Holy Spirit Comes as Oil.

The anointing is directly related to the Holy Spirit's work in our life.[13] His anointing makes us sensitive.[14] How many times have you sensed something was wrong or something was right, but you didn't know why or how you knew? The Holy Spirit, by His anointing and presence, confirms what He is—the Spirit of Truth, of Holiness, of Wisdom. Obeying the Holy Spirit means that He will give us wisdom when we need it in our everyday life.

All the primary offices of Scripture—prophets, priests, and kings—involve anointing. And all of these are offices to which all of us are called. As prophets, we are called to speak the Word of the Lord. As priests, the Lord wants to anoint us for worship. And as kings, we don't just get anointed once and for all. It takes fresh anointing from the Holy Spirit for the dominion of His Kingdom and the authority of His life to happen through us. When it does, we can move in confidence about how to rule our homes and our businesses and how to deal with our kids and our relationships. God's not going to anoint us with the ability to rule when we try to manage things our own way.

The Holy Spirit Comes as Wine.

Ephesians 5:18 draws an analogy for the symbolism of the Holy Spirit as wine. In the Gospels, Jesus describes the new work of God, through the ministry of the Spirit, as new wine coming into old vessels. He pours out His love just like we pour out wine into a glass. We are the vessel, the cup, into whom He pours out his love to inebriate us with his grace. When we have a personal relationship with God in Christ through the Holy Spirit, we experience the love of God. Christianity is an experiential faith, not just an intellectual belief. It is a subjective experience that is full of passion.

The Holy Spirit Comes as Fire.

At Pentecost, the Bible says that tongues that looked like fire appeared over the heads of each of those who gathered together.[15] The Holy Spirit comes as fire to work something deep into the substance of our lives that will shape things around us rather than us taking on the shape of the world. As fire, He works in a dual way: to probe the inner recesses of our life to refine us as gold or silver is refined in fire, and to temper our personalities.

The purifying fire burns out the Adversary. When the three Hebrew children were thrown into the furnace, not only were their lives spared, but also their clothes didn't burn.[16] But the ropes holding them in bondage burned. The Bible speaks of the Holy Spirit being "a spirit of judgment and burning."[17] Judgment has to do with deliverance, in the way the judges of Israel led people out of bondage. The Holy Spirit comes like fire and burns away any grip that the enemy has bound us with.

The Holy Spirit Comes as a Dove.

The Holy Spirit, coming as a dove, is gentle and a symbol of peace. What the dove did is important as well—the dove came and rested on Jesus.[18] The Holy Spirit wants to come and rest upon you and me. Not sweeping throughout the world as a tidal wave of revival, but to come to each of us personally.[19]

He not only administers His gifts, but Holy Spirit empowers the witnesses of the blood and the water. First John 5:6 says, "This is He who came by water and blood—Jesus Christ; not only by water but by water and blood. And it is *the Spirit who bears witness* because the Spirit is truth." These few words describing the Holy Spirit are not even a drop in the bucket of who He is and what He does, but I hope they have piqued your interest in Him.

The Witness of the Blood

I used to ask, "Is there any hope for someone as weak and bound by the kingdom of darkness as I am to experience the blood of Jesus in its full power?" I have learned that just because I have evil spirits bound to me, or I have degrading thoughts, or I act out in shameful ways, the Holy Spirit *still* dwells within me. What a mystery! He didn't bail on me because I sinned or was not yet free. The mistake I made was thinking of the blood as if it bares witness alone. But it is *through the Spirit* that the blood of Jesus has its power, and the Spirit and the blood bear witness *together*. We think of the shedding of

Jesus' blood as an event that occurred two thousand years ago, and then we try to muster up some faith to imagine it as present and real. But, as our faith is always weak, we feel inadequate to do this, and then we have no powerful experience of what the blood can do.

I learned that I was mistaken in my belief that the blood was inactive and needed to be stirred up by my faith to have power. The blood of Jesus is an almighty, eternal power that is always active! When I accepted this truth, then my faith became, for the first time, true faith. I now understand that my weakness cannot interfere with the power of the blood.[20]

Because Holy Spirit is eternal, He makes the blood and the water eternal. Hebrews 9:14 says, "how much more shall the blood of Christ, who *through the eternal Spirit* offered Himself without spot to God, cleanse your conscience from dead works to serve the living God?" The blood possesses its eternal power to cleanse and transform us to serve the living God by the Eternal Spirit who was in Jesus when He shed His blood. This does not mean merely that Holy Spirit was in Jesus and granted Him and His blood a divine worth. It is much more than that! The Eternal Spirit *brought about* the shedding of Jesus' blood, and the Spirit lived and worked in that blood. As a result, when the blood was shed, it could not decay, and as a living substance, it could be taken up to Heaven to exercise its divine power from there.[21]

When we pray for healing, we receive it through the blood of Jesus and the Holy Spirit's administration of the blood. When we ask for power, Holy Spirit is the one who delegates miracle power and authority through all that Jesus accomplished. Since comprehensive teaching on the power of the blood is not the point of this book, what I will say here will barely scratch the surface of its attributes, but I'd like to mention some of them.

1. The blood is alive and eternal.[22]
2. The blood redeems, purchases, cleanses, and keeps you cleansed.[23]
3. The blood releases forgiveness into your life.[24]
4. The blood makes you complete.[25]

5. The blood delivers, destroys the works of darkness, heals, and protects.[26]
6. The blood is eternal.[27]
7. The blood of Jesus Christ speaks.

Wait, what? Blood speaks? That's what Hebrews 12:24 says, "[You have come] to Jesus the Mediator of the new covenant, and to the blood of sprinkling that *speaks better things* than that of Abel."

If you are born again, then the blood of Jesus is speaking on your behalf as a personal character witness to defend your reputation, conduct, and moral nature. And the Bible very clearly says in 1 John 5 that the blood of Jesus is one of those witnesses on this planet.

But that verse in Hebrews twelve that I just mentioned also says that the blood of Jesus speaks better things than that of Abel. I wondered why the author mentioned Abel. Most of us have heard the story about how the first brothers got into a huge fight because Cain (the eldest brother) was jealous of Abel. Jealous because God rejected his sacrifice and accepted Abel's. Cain became furious with his little brother and killed Abel in his rage. Talk about projecting your faults onto someone else! When God questions Cain on the whereabouts of Abel, he replies (to *GOD*, mind you!), "I don't know. Am I my brother's keeper?" And the Lord said, "What have you done? The voice of your brother's blood cries out to Me from the ground."[28] *Blood speaks!*

If you are born again, God has breathed life into you, and His holy oxygen is pumping through your entire being. He has infused your blood and brought it to life; the blood is speaking. So often, when we come to a brick wall ministering to someone to free them from some evil entity, we say, "Lord, You love this person, and I know You want them free. What can we do? What do we say?" Sometimes a spirit is deeply entrenched in their soul, and our authority or anointing is not what will free this person. So we reach for the blood! We loosen the speaking power of the blood of the Lamb and ask the blood to go to that place and speak. Let the blood go beyond where my intellect even knows how to pray because the blood knows how to open every prison door. The blood knows how to find every broken part of the heart; it knows where every bruise and every memory from the past is that still torments them. The blood knows the places where their heart is so hard because of what life has done to them, and suddenly the speaking power of the blood begins to transform them.

The blood will manifest its power in us because the Eternal Spirit of God always works *with it* and *in it*. That, my friend, is the extraordinary witness of the eternal blood!

The Witness of the Water

People are the most surprised by the idea of water as a witness of Jesus Christ. I mean, I get it—it is simply H_2O. But is it *only* H_2O?

Water is by far the most studied chemical compound[29] and is described as the "universal solvent"[30] and the "solvent of life."[31] It is the most abundant substance on the Earth's surface and the only one to exist as a solid, liquid, or gas.[32] It is also the third most abundant molecule in the universe.[33] It's pretty much everywhere, including other planets and moons. So if water is this common, what makes it so special that Apostle John included it along with these other two eternal and holy witnesses?

In terms of water baptism, it's usually a "one and done" kind of thing. Most people do not get water baptized several times. If you're familiar with exorcism practices, then you have probably heard of holy water (used in Roman Catholicism, Eastern Orthodoxy, certain Lutheran synods, Anglicanism, and various other churches).[34] Religiously speaking, though, what else is water good for? Before I studied the Three Witnesses, all of the above just about exhausted my wealth of water knowledge.

When I began to research water as a witness, I was most surprised that I couldn't find any place in the Bible that said it was created. Genesis 1:1-2 says, "In the beginning, God shaped/fashioned the heavens and the earth. The earth was without form and void, and darkness was on the face of the deep (the subterranean waters). And the Spirit of God was hovering over the face of the waters." Hey! Look at that! The Spirit was already in agreement with the witness of the water! He "hovered" over the face of the waters. That word means brooding, fertilizing, or enlivening it. The Spirit cherished the water like a bird broods over her newly laid eggs, suggesting He was protecting the water. Protecting it from what? Well, that's an interesting discussion topic for another day. Maybe even a future book!

Here are some things I have learned about the witness of the water:

The Water Purifies the Body Physically and Symbolically.

In Moses' day, they were required to wash in water before entering the tabernacle.[35]

The Water Covered the Lord's Glory.

"Then the cloud covered the tabernacle of meeting, and the glory of the Lord filled the tabernacle."[36] I was taught my entire life that this was a glory cloud, but it's talking about two different things—a cloud and the Lord's glory. So, before you conclude this is simply a poetic way to describe God's glory, it's important to note what the original Hebrew word here means. It is literally a nimbus or thundercloud.[37] Whoa! Water in one of its three forms—gaseous!

God Turned Water into Blood.

He used Moses' rod to turn the Nile River and all the waters of Egypt into blood to disgrace the Egyptian Nile god Hapi.[38]

The Lord Parted the Red Sea.

"Then Moses raised his hand over the sea, and the Lord opened up a path through the water with a strong east wind." This miraculous act delivered the Israelites from 400 years of slavery and bondage to the Egyptians that day.[39] The Apostle Paul encouraged the church he planted in Corinth, "I don't want you to forget, dear brothers and sisters, about our ancestors in the wilderness long ago. All of them were guided by a cloud that moved ahead of them, and all of them walked through the sea on dry ground. In the cloud and in the sea, all of them were baptized as followers of Moses. All of them ate the same spiritual food, and all of them drank the same spiritual water. For they drank from the spiritual rock that traveled with them, and that rock was Christ."[40]

Waters of Baptism Cleanse Your Conscience.

"Jesus preached to the spirits in prison, those who disobeyed God long ago when God waited patiently while Noah was building his boat. Only eight people were saved from drowning in that terrible flood. And that water is a picture of baptism, which now saves you, not by removing dirt from your body, but as a response to God from a clean conscience. It is effective because of the resurrection of Jesus Christ.[41]

Water is Alive and Eternal.

Jesus said, "but whoever drinks of the water that I shall give him will never thirst. But the water that I shall give him will become in him a fountain of water springing up into everlasting life. He who believes in Me, as the Scripture has said, out of his heart will flow rivers of living water.' But this He spoke concerning the Spirit, whom those believing in Him would receive; for the Holy Spirit was not yet given because Jesus was not yet glorified."[42]

Water is a Big Part of Heaven.

"And he showed me (John) a pure river of water of life, clear as crystal, proceeding from the throne of God and of the Lamb. In the middle of its street, and on either side of the river, was the tree of life, which bore twelve fruits, each tree yielding its fruit every month. The leaves of the tree were for the healing of the nations."[43]

The Water Cleanses Us.

"… Christ also loved the church and gave Himself for her, that He might sanctify and cleanse her with the washing of water by the word, that He might present her to Himself a glorious church, not having spot or wrinkle or any such thing, but that she should be holy and without blemish."[44]

There is so much more we could say about the witness of the water, but let's move on to our next weapon of warfare—severing soul ties.

CHAPTER TWENTY-ONE

Let's Break Some Soul Ties!

As I mentioned in chapter 11, there are all sorts of soul ties. The least complicated definition of a soul tie is an invisible connection, a kind of umbilical cord, between my soul and another person, place, or thing. The tie is anchored in our thoughts, feelings, or choices and the kingdom of darkness uses it to transfer back and forth between each involved party.

We'll begin with a very detailed prayer to break sexual soul ties. My husband conducts a session at a Cleansing Retreat called Pathway to Purity. He teaches what sexual soul ties are and how they are created. Then leads everyone through this prayer. After the prayer, participants are invited to make a list of every individual they have had sex with. Then they are asked to go to a ministry team member who will agree in prayer with them to break each soul tie. This is a very private time, and the lists are destroyed after the prayer. Most people feel a load of guilt drop off their shoulders as Jesus washes them white as snow!

Sexual Soul Tie Prayer

This is the Pathway to Purity prayer:

Heavenly Father, I come to you in the name of your son and my savior Jesus Christ. I believe the blood of Jesus is all-powerful and can cleanse me from all sin. I desire freedom from all filth of a sexual nature, which has come to me through my eyes, ears, mind, and actual participation in sin.

On behalf of my forefathers and myself, I repent of all affections for and attachments to philosophies, religions, and lifestyles that glorify, promote, or condone sexual conduct contrary to God's holy Word. I specifically confess as sin, repent and renounce all spirits of sexual lust. This includes lust of the eyes, lust of the flesh, sexual fantasies, impure thoughts, lewdness, and obsession with the physical body.

I repent for sexual sins committed outside of marriage, such as petting and oral sex. I repent and renounce the demons behind addiction to sexual self-gratification, including compulsive masturbation.

I repent of all involvement in pornography. I renounce the spirits behind pornographic photos, art, and drawings. I renounce the spirits behind pornographic novels, books, magazines, movies, television, videos, and internet sites. I renounce the production, sale, and distribution of pornographic material. I repent and renounce the spirits behind adultery, betrayal, infidelity, and fornication.

I repent and renounce spirits associated with all known or unknown forms of sexual perversion, including anal sex, sex with demons, exhibitionism, indecent exposure, bestiality, rape, child molestation, homosexuality, lesbianism, and sodomy.

I repent of all my attitudes and actions and renounce the spirits behind sexual pride, sexual conquest, sexual power over others, flirting, enticement, seduction, and all forms of manipulation.

I repent of all involvement with abortions and renounce the spirits of murder, death, selfishness, and rejection of children. I renounce all human sacrifice demons. In Jesus' name, I break any curses of death over my family.

Father God, I repent of rebelling against your divine instructions and giving place to any spirit that would bind, control, or manipulate me. I renounce eye control spirits, mind control spirits, dream control spirits, sexually enticing dreams, filthy dreams, tormenting dreams. I renounce memory recall spirits, entrapping spirits, seducing spirits, and spirits that would inform me of the sexual availability in others. I renounce every controlling and possessive spirit.

I also repent of giving place to spirits that would bring fear. I renounce fear of intimacy, fear of sex in marriage, fear of not measuring up, fear of being violated, fear of being used, fear of being abandoned, and all spirits of frigidity.

I believe that Jesus Christ died on the cross for me, so I appropriate Galatians 3:13, which says He paid the price and became a curse for me. Jesus nailed to the cross all the handwritings that Satan has against me. And so I declare all curses over my life, whether through my sexual sin or those of my ancestors, to be broken. I renounce all the works of the kingdom of darkness, and as I break soul ties with past sexual partners, I command that every sexual spirit that has a foothold in my life will be gone, depart, and leave me in the name of Jesus Christ.

So, Father God, I ask you now to remind me of every person I have sinned with sexually, for it is my will that all the emotional, mental, and physical ties be broken now.[1]

Phew! I told you it was detailed! Now make your list of sexual partners. You should review Chapter 6 of this book to help you make a thorough list. Let me suggest a few things that we've encountered over the years:

1. If you are married and had sex with your spouse before marriage, that's an unholy tie. Be sure to put your spouse's name on your list because God wants that broken.

2. We ministered to a woman who had been raped in a specific house for many years. As an adult, she could not get over the torment of that house, and she saw it all the time in her memory and her dreams. The Holy Spirit told her to sever ties with the house, so she did. She was instantly freed from that torment! I can't take you to a scripture that says sever ties with houses but if God instructs you to break a soul tie to a location, then just do it.

3. We ministered to a man who couldn't get the pictures off his mind from a specific pornographic magazine that he had looked at for years. He wrote down the particular name of that magazine and broke ties to it. Once he broke ties to the magazine, all those pictures went away.

Now, make a list of every individual you have had sex with. Don't feel intimidated by this exercise. If you can't remember someone's name, then describe them to the best of your ability, "the guy with the cool Firebird." After you finish your list, then use this prayer as an outline and mention each name individually:

1. Lord, I repent for sexual sin with _____.
2. I renounce every spirit that came to me through that soul tie.
3. I break that soul tie now, in Jesus' Name.

This same prayer outline can be used to break any type of soul tie. This includes if you have used a Ouija Board and need to break the tie to the board's spirit master and/or the person who owns the board. In that case, you would repent for the sin of seeking knowledge from the spirit realm rather than from God.

If you find yourself pondering, "Hmmmmmmm… I wonder if I have a soul tie to _____?" Don't spend any time trying to solve the mystery. Just assume you do, pray and break the soul tie.

CHAPTER TWENTY-TWO

Casting Out Nephilim

Why did I talk about the Three Witnesses before explaining how to cast out Nephilim? As I've said, the Bible is a spiritual treasure chest filled with supernatural tools. If you choose to view them all symbolically, then so be it to you according to your faith. But the Word tells us that God's people are destroyed because they lack knowledge.[1] I want to turn that around, don't you? The enemy is destroyed because God's people possess eternal knowledge!

The Earth was corrupt before God and was filled with violence, for all flesh had corrupted their way on the planet.[2] How did they corrupt their way? Having sex with rebellious angels and birthing Nephilim spoiled the human race. And it wasn't sin that was the problem. God had a plan to deal with sin and redemption. Jesus' death on the cross and resurrection would conquer sin. No, this was different. The human race had been infected with Nephilim. This was Satan's plan to pollute the lineage from which Jesus would come. But Noah found grace in the eyes of the Lord because he was a just man, perfect in his generations.[3] Meaning there were no Nephilim in his family through which the Messiah would come.

Skip ahead a few thousand years when Jesus told His disciples that just as it was in the days of Noah, so it will be at the end of time—*that means now!*[4] This saying can be interpreted to mean several things, but two things stand out about the days of Noah: Nephilim and water. How did God destroy the giants? He used a *lot* of water! He instructed Noah to build the ark, and then God flooded the Earth.

We are often asked, "How do I know if I have a Nephilim tormenting me?" Even though the example I used in chapter twelve was of a Nephilim who raped me, they are not only sexual creatures. If you often become overwhelmed by your emotions in a way that feels "over the top," you could be bound by a Nephilim. They are giants, and they tend to cause "giant" emotions or feelings of being out of control. They can do this with your thoughts, causing you to obsess over something or someone, or they can cause your thoughts to race out of control.

The Process to Cast Out Nephilim

1. We always begin with repentance. I repent for all ancestral and personal sin—those that I can remember and those that I can't remember—that has given this Nephilim the legal right to be bound to my soul.

2. As it was in the days of Noah, I flood this Nephilim with the Witness of the Water. May the water completely fill the space in my soul where this being is attached.

3. I break soul ties with every person you are attached to.

4. I renounce you, Nephilim. I remove your legal right to stay.

5. I command you to leave me now, in Jesus' Name.

CHAPTER TWENTY-THREE

Freedom From Unclean Spirits

Is it possible to be freed from unclean spirits? If so, how do we do it? The good news is, yes, we can be freed from unclean spirits just as we can be freed from any other type of spirit. But, move around in deliverance ministry long enough, and you'll hear someone say, "Be careful about casting out demons. They can come back seven times worse!" This peculiar belief causes many to avoid even the subject of deliverance and the possibility of freedom. I suppose they conclude it's better to be a little tormented than to risk getting more than they already have.

I made up my mind years ago that I would never decide to do or not do something based on fear. So the first time I heard this deliverance caution, I had to dive in deeply to get an understanding. The specific bible passage about which many people are confused is found in the Books of Matthew and Luke. Jesus taught, "When an unclean spirit goes out of a man, he goes through dry places, seeking rest, and finds none. Then he says, 'I will return to my house from which I came.' And when he comes, he finds it empty, swept, and put in order. Then he goes and takes seven other spirits more wicked than himself, and they enter and dwell there, and the last state of that man is worse than the first."[1] The first point of confusion is the misunderstanding that unclean spirits are just another term for demons, which we know is incorrect. The second point of confusion is that Jesus is not talking about casting an unclean spirit out of someone. He explains the journey of an unclean spirit who *chooses* to astral project out of the host to whom he's bound. The Greek word (*exerchomai*)² for *goes out* has the same meaning as in Matthew 13:1, "On the same day Jesus *went out* of the house and sat by the sea." Though the unclean spirit can go out of their host and wander around, he cannot stay out. He must return to the host because his silver cord is still attached to that person.

Once again, yes, we can be freed from unclean spirits. Matthew 10:1 says, "And when He had called His twelve disciples to Him, He gave them power over unclean spirits, to cast them out." To *cast out* is the Greek word *ekballō*,³ an entirely different word than exerchomai.

Now for the second question: How are we freed from unclean spirits? Because he explains it better than anyone I know, here's an excerpt from Timothy's book, *Unclean Spirits: One of Satan's Best-Kept Secrets*.⁴

Let me take you back to 1989… I was in a major battle. I was worn out. This "thing" declares, "You can't cast me out because I am a person." As soon as the spirit said that, my mind began to replay information I had accumulated concerning the subject of transference of human spirits.

Silently in my spirit, I began to talk to God. "If what other people have said, and if this spirit is speaking the truth, then God, I do not know what to do."

Those moments seemed like forever. I sat there praying with this "person" looking at me in all their pride. I could sense they saw my confusion and that I was scrambling. And all of a sudden, boom! It became clear. When God dropped the revelation into my mind of what to do, it was as real as if someone walked up behind me and smacked the back of my head. My mind had just received revelation from the Spirit of the Living God. Instantly I saw a picture of Jesus on the Cross. He had been there a few hours, and it was the moment He looked up and said, "Father, into Your hands, I commit my spirit," and then He breathed His last.⁵ My computer brain processed this revelation; I looked this person in the eye and said, "I repeat the words that my Savior spoke on the Cross, into the Father's hands, I commit your spirit."

Instantly the pride and arrogance was gone! "Who told you that?" they exclaimed as panic began to set in. And for the first time in this battle, we were winning. I instantly knew we had the upper hand. I continued to press in.

"This is not your house, not your tabernacle. You are not to be here. It is God's will that you are gone. Now, into the Father's hands, I commit your spirit."

At this point in the battle, the person's pupils became big and dilated. They intently looked over my shoulder, struggling to see who had just entered the room. What they were glaring at, I did not see. But I felt the presence, and I knew the Word of God. I knew what was happening. The Word teaches that when a person is about to "die," angels arrive to escort them to Abraham's bosom or hell.[6] When does death occur? As we already discussed, when the "silver cord" is severed.

Without a pause in the battle, I found myself praying, "Father, I break every soul tie, every spirit tie, every human spirit tie. I sever their cord of life, and into the Father's hands, I commit this spirit. Be gone!" They left without any coughing and simply a long exhale of a breath.

The Process to Cast Out Unclean Spirits

Have you ever heard someone say a threefold cord is not easily broken? That's because it's a spiritual law, and we find it in Ecclesiastes 4:12. In my personal experience, I have observed that *every* time we encounter an unclean spirit, there are demons with it. And most of the time, there are also Nephilim. I see a demon, a Nephilim, and an unclean spirit as a demonic threefold cord.

Since each one is defeated differently, it has been easy for them to win most of their battles. A person may think they are battling a demon when it is actually a Nephilim or an unclean spirit. This fight can go on for hours because the enemy sends up other types of beings when one begins to wear out.

1. We always begin with repentance. I repent for all ancestral and per-

sonal sins—those that I can remember and those that I can't remember—that have given this unclean spirit the legal right to be bound to my soul.

2. According to 1 John 5:8, there are three eternal witnesses on Earth: the Spirit, the water, and the blood. So I flood this unclean spirit with the witness of the water. May the water completely fill the space in my soul where this spirit is attached.

3. I renounce you, spirit. I sever your silver cord and remove your legal right to stay.

4. Into the Father's hands, I commit your spirit. I command you to leave me now, in Jesus' Name.

EPILOGUE

My Secret Is Out!

*Nothing in the world is more dangerous
then a sincere ignorance and conscientious stupidity.*
Martin Luther King, Jr.

Well, my secret is out, and no one died! There *are* invisible entities that dwell in the dark, and *they are fearsome*. But don't be afraid—they can be defeated! My exchanges with the spirit world may be extreme; however, they are merely a sampling of a lifetime of experiences.

Over the years, I have talked with many peers and various professionals about what I see. I have spoken with members of the clergy, Jewish scholars, psychologists, and others who see spirit beings. I was given a variety of conflicting explanations, and more than one person warned me never to talk about this subject again because, I quote, "they will surely diagnose you as psychotic and lock you up." This was when I concluded that people fear what they do not understand, and to avoid the fear, they must believe it is not real. Martin Luther King's term was "conscientious stupidity." Ignorance of a subject is one thing, but to choose ignorance is pure stupidity.

C.S. Lewis's book *The Screwtape Letters* is a satirical novel featuring Screwtape, a senior demon of the "Lowerarchy," who writes 31 letters to his novice nephew with advice on how to win the soul of a young man and keep him from "the Enemy" (i.e., God). Screwtape explains how the kingdom of darkness persuades humans to choose ignorance of Satan and his evil workers.

He said, "It is funny how mortals always picture us putting things into their minds: in reality, our best work is done by *keeping things out*...Our policy, for the moment, is to conceal ourselves...I do not think you will have much difficulty in keeping the patient in the dark. The fact that 'devils' are predominately comic figures in the modern imagination will help you. If any faint suspicion of your existence begins to arise in his mind, suggest to him a picture of something in red tights, and persuade him that since he cannot believe in that (it is an old textbook method of confusing them), he, therefore, cannot believe in you."

If you see what I see, I hope you realize now that you're not strange, abnormal, or cursed. You are peculiar, but I mean that in the most complimentary way. The Word of God tells us that Jesus purifies for Himself a peculiar people.[1] It means we are specifically selected, and He enables you to do something about what you see in the spirit realm. The world, and specifically the Church of Jesus Christ, needs you! You are not a victim of evil; you are a survivor of it. Each person has choices to make and boundaries they can enforce with demons, human spirits, and Nephilim. I know this to be true because I have learned the spiritual laws that enable us to live peacefully in this world and, more importantly, *victoriously* in it. I hope that what I've learned helps you.

I have also discovered that when we find meaning in our suffering, it becomes tolerable, and its purpose is powerful. My experience seeing and interacting with the spirit world was less painful once I realized I could use it to help others, partly by writing this book. Life is sweeter when we understand how our pain has positively contributed to our progress and it can inspire others.

If you have questions or are tormented by a spirit and don't know what to do, please get in touch with me at doyousee.org. I hope what I have learned thus far on my journey will help you on yours. The things that have happened to you do not define you. Who you are today and who you will become tomorrow is grace's definition of you.

But in case I have led you to believe that I am the main character of this book, I want to correct that message unequivocally. The hero of my story is and always will be my friend, Jesus. He was there in the beginning, even when I was a terrified and confused little girl. He is still the one who faithfully takes my hand when I'm not feeling brave enough to face pain and uncertainty. And I know He'll be in all my tomorrows because He promises me He will.

* * *

If I go up to the heavens, you are there;
if I make my bed in the depths, you are there.
If I rise on the wings of the dawn, if I settle on the far side of the sea,
even there your hand will guide me, your right hand will hold me fast.
If I say, "Surely the darkness will hide me
and the light become night around me,"
even the darkness will not be dark to you;
the night will shine like the day, for darkness is as light to you.
For you created my inmost being;
you knit me together in my mother's womb.
I praise you because I am fearfully and wonderfully made;
your works are wonderful, I know that full well.
My frame was not hidden from you when I was made in the secret place,
when I was woven together in the depths of the Earth.
Your eyes saw my unformed body; all the days ordained for me
were written in your book before one of them came to be.
How precious to me are your thoughts, God!
How vast is the sum of them!
Were I to count them, they would outnumber the grains of sand—
when I awake, *You are still with me!*

King David, c. 6th Century BCE
Psalm 139:8-18 NIV

Acknowledgments

I wish to thank my husband, Timothy, who supports me, always. It was easy to know to whom to dedicate this book, which I have been writing for about twenty years. The process began with the Chapter One story, a memory long since suppressed, unfolding verbatim early one morning precisely as it is written. This memory opened the door to most of the others, but not without much travail and torment. Thankfully, Timothy was always available to pray for me, fight for me, and love me through the good, the bad, and the really bad.

I am grateful to my parents for believing in me and trusting that my spiritual sight comes from God. I can't imagine what it must have been like to raise me! God knew just whom to choose for that task; they are the exact mom and dad I needed. I am very thankful they raised me to have a loving relationship with Jesus because that's what has carried me through. I am also grateful for Kim, who has had to endure life as my little sister. Her love and faith in me surpass my comprehension.

Finally, during the writing of this book, life at our house was sometimes strained. But our children have always been more than encouraging and became my personal cheer squad. I am forever grateful to them.

Bibles That Name Archangels

I realize it can sound as if I'm intolerant or judgmental of these sacred texts, but I would like to remind you that in Chapter Two, I state that I wholeheartedly trust the Christian Bible because I've seen it in action. Its laws are the only ones that actually affect the kingdom of darkness. So, we can safely say that I am biased toward the Protestant Christian Bible. To be thorough, I mention the five other bibles that include angels in their script. I know… this part seems a bit textbookish to me, too, but here it is:

Jewish Hebrew Bible[1]

Contains 39 books written originally in Hebrew and divided into three parts: The Law, The Prophets, and The Writings.

Catholic and Orthodox Christian Bible[2]

Contains 73 books divided into two parts: the Old Testament and the New Testament.

Old Testament: all 39 books of the Jewish Hebrew Bible plus seven books added by Roman Catholic law (called apocryphal books by the Protestants).

New Testament: 27 books written originally in Greek recording the life and teachings of Jesus and his earliest followers, as well as events in first-century Christianity.

Protestant Christian Bible[3]

Contains 66 books, including all of the Catholic and Orthodox Christian Bible, but *excluding* the seven apocryphal books.

Mormon Bible (LDS)[4]

Members of The Church of Jesus Christ of Latter-day Saints (or "Mormons") have four books that are considered part of the church's official canon. These books are often collectively referred to as the "standard works" of the church: the Bible (a church-produced King James Version with Mormon annotations is the preferred version), *The Book of Mormon*, *The Doctrine and Covenants*, and *The Pearl of Great Price*. Generally speaking, Mormons understand scripture as encompassing these four "standard works" and official pronouncements and sermons by general authorities of the church.

Ethiopian Orthodox Bible[5]

[WARNING! *This one is confusing*]

The Orthodox Tewahedo biblical canon is a version of the Christian Bible used in the two Oriental Orthodox churches of the Ethiopian and Eritrean traditions: the Ethiopian Orthodox Tewahedo Church and the Eritrean Orthodox Tewahedo Church. At 81 books, it is the largest and most diverse biblical canon in traditional Christendom.

Western scholars have classified the books of the canon into two categories—the narrower canon, which consists mostly of books familiar to the West, and the broader canon, which includes nine additional books.

Old Testament: The Orthodox Tewahedo narrower Old Testament canon contains the entire established Hebrew protocanon (books also included in the Hebrew Bible). Moreover, except for the first two books of Maccabees, the Orthodox Tewahedo canon also contains the entire Catholic deuterocanon. In addition, the Orthodox Tewahedo Old Testament includes the Prayer of Manasseh, 3 Ezra, and 4 Ezra, which also appear in the canons of other Christian traditions (*not* the Protestant Christian Bible). Unique to the Orthodox Tewahedo canon are the Paralipomena of Jeremiah (4 Baruch), Jubilees, Enoch, and the three books of Meqabyan. The books of Lamentations, Jeremiah and Baruch, as well as the Letter of Jeremiah and 4 Baruch, are all considered canonical by the Orthodox Tewahedo churches. Additionally, the 1st, 2nd, and 3rd Books of Ethiopian Maccabees are also part of the canon; while they share a common name, they are entirely different from the books of Maccabees that are known or have been canonized in other traditions. Finally, within the Orthodox Tewahedo tradition, 3 Ezra is called Second Ezra, 4 Ezra is called Ezra Sutu'el, and the Prayer of Manasseh is incorporated into the Second Book of Chronicles.

New Testament: The Orthodox Tewahedo narrower New Testament canon consists of the 27-book Protestant Christian New Testament.

One published compilation of the Ethiopian Orthodox Bible is not known to exist at this time.

Islamic Bible, Quran[6]

The language of the Quran is Arabic. It is a compilation of the verbal revelations given to the Prophet Muhammad over twenty-three years. It is divided into 114 chapters. The chapters, called Surah in Arabic, are of varying lengths, some consisting of a few lines while others run for many pages.

APPENDIX II

Names of Archangels

Kabbalah, Jewish mysticism based on the books of Zohar, names ten archangels: Metatron, Raziel, Tzaphkiel, Zadkiel, Chamuel, Michael, Raphael, Haniel, Gabriel, and Sandalphon.

Besides Michael, Daniel mentions the angel Gabriel by name. I have heard and read innumerable references to Gabriel as the Archangel Gabriel. However, he is never given that title in the Hebrew Bible or the Christian Bible. In fact, he is not given any title. Many scholars consider him one of the angel princes or chiefs of angels. Though he never acted as a warrior, he always delivered personal messages from God to people.

The Catholic Bible names three archangels: Michael, Gabriel, and Raphael. The Eastern Catholic Church believes there are thousands of archangels, but only seven are given names: Michael, Gabriel, Raphael, Uriel, Jeremiel, Salathiel, and Phaltiel (or Psaltiel).

Once founded in Jewish and Christian bibles, today, Islamic beliefs are based solely on the writings of the Quran. The archangels named in the Quran are Michael, Gabriel, Raphael, and Azrael.

The occult/paganism petitions the help of archangels on a regular basis. Because the terms occult and paganism may conjure negative ideas for some, I will define them as magical or supernatural arts or influences. Their practices consist of a mixed bag of tricks, including astrology, Zodiac, Tarot cards, ritual magic, and worship of various gods and goddesses, to name a few. Pagan archangels are associated with high magic, and their duties are to protect and support people. Some say there are at least four and as many as twenty-six archangels. Most groups name Michael, Gabriel, Raphael, Uriel, Raguel, Remiel, Sariel, and Lucifer. A few groups include Satan as an archangel. The belief is that each archangel has specific powers or abilities and, excluding Satan, can impart virtues such as courage, conception, grace, peace, strength, physical healing, and many others—if only we call upon them for help. Each archangel is connected to an aura color and crystal stone. For instance, it is accepted that Archangel Michael's aura is royal blue mixed with royal purple and his crystal stone is sugilite. Archangels also oversee seasons, days of the week, elements such as wind and fire, and planets.[199]

Now let's consider the Book of Enoch. This is not currently a belief or philosophy, but I include it because I see a trend moving in that direction, especially among some Christian groups. The Book of Enoch, written during the second century BCE, is considered by Yale Library as one of the most important non-canonical pseudepigraphical works. Its only complete extant version is an Ethiopic translation of a Greek translation made in Palestine from the original Hebrew or Aramaic. Enoch, the great-grandfather of Noah and the seventh patriarch in the book of Genesis, is one of the two people in the Bible taken up to heaven without dying (the other being Elijah) and the subject of abundant apocalyptic literature. At first revered only for his piety, he was later believed to be the recipient of secret knowledge from God, which manifests in the Book of Enoch's concepts of heaven and hell, angels and demons, the messiah, the resurrection, a final judgment, and a heavenly kingdom on Earth.[200] The part that should be a red flag to anyone who can do simple math, is that Noah and Enoch lived approximately 2,000 years before the book was written. Though it is a Jewish text, every other canonical bible but one excludes it—that bible is the Ethiopian Orthodox Bible. The Book of Enoch mentions multitudes of angels by name, including archangels and several of what it classifies as the 199 fallen angels that impregnated human women, resulting in Nephilim offspring. The archangels named in this book are Michael, Gabriel, Raphael, and Uriel.

The Greek God Pan

The culture of Ancient Greece involved a complex spiritual world of major and minor gods that oversaw human events and engaged in dramas of their own. One of these, called Pan, ruled over nature and pastureland, and he is frequently depicted in literature and artworks. Although he is not one of the major gods of Ancient Greece, he is one of the most often-referenced figures in Greek mythology.

Pan, the God of the Wild

Pan is considered to be one of the oldest Greek gods. He is associated with nature, wooded areas, and pastureland, from which his name is derived. The worship of Pan began in rural areas far from the populated city centers. Because of this, he did not have prominent temples built to worship him. Instead, worship of Pan centered in nature, often in caves or grottoes. Pan ruled over shepherds, hunters, and rustic music. He was the patron god of Arcadia. Pan was often in the company of the wood nymphs and other forest deities.

Pan's Appearance

Perhaps because of his association with nature and animals, the bottom half of Pan's body was like a goat, with the top half being like a man. However, he is often depicted with horns on his head, and his face is usually unattractive.

Pan's Lineage

The parentage of Pan is uncertain. Some accounts say he is the son of Hermes[1] and Dryope, but others say he is the son of Zeus[2] or Penelope, the wife of Odysseus. His birth story says that his mother was so distressed by his unusual appearance that she ran away, but he was taken to Mount Olympus, where he became the gods' favorite.

Pan's Powers

Like the other gods of Olympus, Pan possessed enormous strength. He could also run for long periods and was impervious to injury. He could transform objects into different forms and teleport himself from Earth to Mount Olympus and back. He is depicted as very shrewd with a wonderful sense of humor.

Pan and Music

The mythological stories involving Pan usually involve his romantic interest in a lovely goddess of the woods who spurns his advances and gets turned into an inanimate object to escape him or who otherwise flees from his ugly appearance. One story concerns Syrinx, a beautiful wood nymph. She flees from Pan's attentions, and her fellow goddesses turn her into a river reed to hide her from him. They make a gentle musical sound as the winds blow through the reeds. Because he does not know which reed Syrinx is, he cuts several reeds from the group and sets them in a line to make the musical instrument, the pan flute. Pan's image is often depicted with this instrument.

Pan Gave Humans the Word "Panic"

One story involving Pan is the tale of war, in which Pan helps his friend survive a vicious struggle by letting out a big cry that frightens the enemy and causes him to run away. From this story, we get the word "panic," the sudden, uncontrollable fear that leads people into irrational behavior.

Pan in the Modern World

Over the ages, Pan has been a symbol of the force of nature. In the 1800s, interest in this mythological figure revived, and communities organized festivals where Pan was the central figure. Mythical stories of Pan's antics abound, and he continues to represent the ancient mystery of the forest, hunting activities, and wildlife.

Like the other gods of Ancient Greece, Pan embodies many qualities of the world over which he ruled. He is depicted as energetic, sometimes frightening, with the wild, unbridled creative force of nature, making him an exciting and often entertaining character.[3]

Notes

PROLOGUE
1. Matthew 28:19.
2. John 10:10.
3. Isaiah 45:3.
4. Ephesians 1:17-18.

CHAPTER ONE: MY OWN PERSONAL DRAGON
1. Exodus 20:5, Deuteronomy 5:9.

CHAPTER TWO: ANGELS AMONGST US
1. See Appendix I for a list of these bibles and sacred texts.
2. "H4397 - mal'ak - Strong's Hebrew Lexicon (kjv)." Blue Letter Bible. Web. 17 June, 2019. <https://www.blueletterbible.org/lexicon/h4397/kjv/wlc/0-1/>.
3. Ezekiel 28:14.
4. "H1966 - hêlel - Strong's Hebrew Lexicon (kjv)." Blue Letter Bible. Web.17 June, 2019. <https://www.blueletterbible.org/lexicon/h1966/kjv/wlc/0-1/>.
5. John 1:9.
6. Isaiah 14:13-14.
7. Revelation 12:4.
8. Genesis 2:17.
9. Genesis 3:24.
10. Phaedo, 108.
11. Learnreligions.com, s.v. "Angels of the Quran," accessed January 12, 2021, https://www.learnreligions.com/angels-of-the-quran-124015
12. Genesis 19:1.
13. Jude 1:9.
14. See Appendix II for a list of archangel names found in other writings.
15. Matthew 2:11, Mark 1:13, Luke 22:43.

16. Mark 1:13.
17. Luke 22: 42-43.
18. 1 Kings 19:3-8.
19. Psalm 91:11, Matthew 18:10.
20. Preachitteachit.org, s.v. "Guardian Angels," accessed January 30, 2021, https://preachitteachit.org/articles/detail/i-met-my-daughters-guardian-angel/.
21. Psalm 91:11-12, Luke 4:10-11

CHAPTER THREE: DEMENTED DEMONS

1. E. N. Aron, "Reasons From Our Past For Ranking Ourselves Too Low," in The Undervalued Self (New York: Little, Brown and Company, 2010): 78-79.
2. 1 Corinthians 6:18.
3. Matthew 12:24.
4. Merriam-Webster.com, s.v. "Morality", accessed January 23, 2021, https://www.merriam-webster.com/dictionary/morality.
5. Merriam-Webster.com, s.v. "Sin", accessed January 23, 2021, https://www.merriam-webster.com/dictionary/sin.
6. Wikipedia.org, s.v. "Sin", accessed January 23, 2021, https://en.wikipedia.org/wiki/Sin.
7. Verywellmind.com, s.v. "Nature versus nurture", accessed January 23, 2021, https://www.verywellmind.com/what-is-nature-versus-nurture-2795392.
8. Ephesians 2:2.
9. Luke 3:38.
10. Genesis 1:27.
11. Genesis 2:7.
12. Genesis 2:16-17.
13. Genesis 5:3.
14. John 3:6-7.
15. Romans 3:23.
16. Romans 5:12.
17. Romans 5:18.
18. Ephesians 4:26-27.
19. T. C. Davis, "Cleansing: Session Four," in The Cleansing Seminar, 1987, n.p.
20. 2 Corinthians 10:5.
21. Genesis 3:1-24.

22. G5117 - topos - Strong's Greek Lexicon (NKJV). Blue Letter Bible. Accessed November 14, 2022. https://www.blueletterbible.org/lexicon/g5117/nkjv/tr/0-1/.
23. T. C. Davis, "Cleansing: Session Four," in The Cleansing Seminar, 1987, n.p.
24. Wonderopolis.org, s.v. "How Many Times Does Your Heart Beat In A Lifetime?", accessed June 21, 2018, https://wonderopolis.org/wonder/how-many-times-does-your-heart-beat-in-a-lifetime.
25. Plato.stanford.edu, s.v. "Plato," accessed May 20, 2011, http://plato.stanford.edu/entries/plato/.
26. Romans 10:10.
27. T. C. Davis, "Cleansing: Session Four," in The Cleansing Seminar, 1987, n.p.

CHAPTER FOUR: FACING THE DARKNESS
1. Hosea 4:6

CHAPTER FIVE: DEBRIEFING THE DEMONIC IN THE DORM ROOM
1. Deuteronomy 30:19.
2. Anomalien.com, s.v. "Word Curses," accessed June 7, 2018, https://anomalien.com/learn-black-magick-curse-your-enemy-in-4-easy-steps/.
3. Spanish writer and author of 'El Quijote, 1547-1616.
4. Galatians 6:7.

CHAPTER SIX: MY SOUL TO KEEP
1. Matthew 6:21, Luke 12:34.
2. The Harris Poll.com, s.v. "Do people believe spirits survive after death," accessed May 17, 2021, https://theharrispoll.com/though-americans-are-currently-attempting-to-recover-from-their-halloween-sugar-comas-with-our-presidential-election-looming-religious-beliefs-are-rising-to-the-tops-of-many-conversations-and-minds/.

CHAPTER SEVEN: TIES THAT BIND
1. Exodus 20:2-17 and Deuteronomy 5:6-21.
2. Reuters.com, s.v. "Have people heard of the ten commandments," accessed February 2, 2021, https://www.reuters.com/article/us-bible-commandments/americans-know-big-macs-better-than-ten-commandments-idUSN1223894020071012.

3. John 20:31, Acts 4:12.
4. Mark 1:27.
5. To purchase this ebook by Timothy Davis, go to https://www.amazon.com/UNCLEAN-SPIRITS-Satans-Best-Kept-Secrets-ebook/.
6. See Appendix III to learn more about Pan.
7. Malachi 4:5-6.
8. Matthew 16:13-20.
9. Luke 9:28-31 (NLT).
10. Matthew 17:3, Mark 9:4.

CHAPTER EIGHT: THE UNDERWORLD

1. Revelation 20:15.
2. 2 Peter 2:4.
3. Jude 6:9.
4. Luke 16:19-31 (NET); "G86 - hades - Strong's Greek Lexicon (nkjv)." Blue Letter Bible. Web. 8 Jan, 2023. <https://www.blueletterbible.org/lexicon/g86/nkjv/tr/0-1/>.
5. Luke 23:42-43 (NLT); "G3857 - paradeisos - Strong's Greek Lexicon (nkjv)." Blue Letter Bible. Web. 8 Jan, 2023. <https://www.blueletterbible.org/lexicon/g3857/nkjv/tr/0-1/>.
6. Matthew 12:40.
7. Matthew 5:22.
8. 2 Kings 2:11 (NLT).
9. Versebyverseministry.org, s.v. "Where did Elijah go when he was taken up," accessed February 7, 2021, https://www.versebyverseministry.org/bible-answers/where-did-god-take-elijah-and-when-did-it-happen.
10. John 3:13.
11. Mark 9:2-10, Matthew 17:1-8, Luke 9:28-33.
12. Luke 23:46.
13. Matthew 12:40 (NLT).
14. 1 Peter 3:18-19.
15. Hebrews 11:39-40.
16. Revelation 1:18.
17. Ephesians 4:8-10.
18. 1 Corinthians 15:20.
19. Matthew 27:52-53.
20. John 20:17 (NLT).
21. Hebrews 9:11-12.

22. Matthew 27:52-53.
23. John 20:27.
24. 2 Corinthians 12:4, Revelation 2:7.

CHAPTER NINE: THE UNREST OF THE UNDEAD
1. 2 Corinthians 5:6-8.
2. Merriam-Webster.com, s.v. "Murder", accessed April 4, 2017, https://www.merriam-webster.com/dictionary/murder.
3. Exodus 20:13.
4. Merriam-Webster.com, s.v. "Revenge", accessed April 4, 2017, https://www.merriam-webster.com/dictionary/revenge.
5. Deuteronomy 32:35.
6. Merriam-Webster.com, s.v. "Obsession", accessed April 4, 2017, https://www.merriam-webster.com/dictionary/obsession.
7. Brontë, Emily, 1818-1848. Wuthering Heights. London ; New York :Penguin Books, 2003.
8. Gesenius's Hebrew and Chaldee Lexicon.
9. S.v. "Ghosts", accessed November 19, 2022.
10. Ibid.
11. Merriam-Webster.com, s.v. "Haunt", accessed December 18, 2021, https://www.merriam-webster.com/dictionary/haunt.
12. Genesis 4:10; Numbers 19:14-16, 22; Isaiah 6:5; Amos 7:17.
13. Gen. 4:10; Numbers 19:14-16, 22; Is. 6:5; Amos 7:17.
14. Matthew 10:1; Mark 1:27, 3:11, 5:13, 6:7; Luke 4:36, 6:18; Acts 5:16, 8:7.
15. Yivoencyclopedia.org, s.v. "Dybbuk", accessed December 18, 2021, https://yivoencyclopedia.org/article.aspx/Possession_and_Exorcism.
16. En.wikipedia.org, s.v. "Ghost", accessed December 18, 2021, https://en.wikipedia.org/wiki/Bhoot_(ghost).
17. A mantle is a sleeveless outer garment worn by men of rank and identified to whom it belonged.
18. 1 Samuel 15:23-28.
19. 1 Samuel 28:3-20.
20. 1 Samuel 31:1-6.
21. Nanai people in Siberia.
22. The Shaman: Patterns of Religious Healing Among the Ojibway Indians, by John A. Grim.
23. Medium.com, s.v. "Balinese Hinduism ancestral spirits", accessed Novem-

ber 19, 2022, https://medium.com/@tribalingual/ghostly-traditions-monsters-and-spirits-from-the-balinese-culture-cb01d32676a8.
24. Galatians 3:13.
25. Exodus 20:5, 34:7; Numbers 14:18; Deuteronomy 5:9.26. 2 Peter 3:9.

CHAPTER ELEVEN: DISSEVER MY SOUL
1. Genesis 34:1-3 (KJV).
2. Blueletterbible.org, s.v. "Clave", accessed June 21, 2011, https://www.blueletterbible.org/lang/lexicon/lexicon.cfm?Strongs=H1692&t=KJV.
3. Urbandictionary.com, s.v. "Psychic Connections," accessed January 27, 2021, https://www.urbandictionary.com/define.php?term=psychic%20connection.
4. Blueletterbible.org, s.v. "Fornication," accessed January 27, 2021, https://www.blueletterbible.org/lang/lexicon/lexicon.cfm?Strongs=G4202&t=NLT.
5. Busypastorsermons.com, s.v. "Church of Corinth," accessed January 27, 2021, https://www.busypastorsermons.com/what-were-the-problems-in-the-corinthian-church/.
6. 1 Corinthians 6:15-17 (NLT).
7. Dictionary.com, s.v. "Covenant," accessed June 21, 2018, https://www.dictionary.com/browse/covenant?s=t.
8. H. Clay Trumbull, The Blood Covenant (John D. Wattles & Co., 1898), 5-6.
9. Wikipedia.org, s.v. "Palo," accessed November 25, 2022, https://en.wikipedia.org/wiki/Palo_(religion).
10. Medlineplus.org, s.v. "What does DNA stand for," accessed November 25, 2022, https://medlineplus.gov/genetics/understanding/basics/dna/.
11. John 10:10.

CHAPTER THIRTEEN: GIANTS IN THE LAND
1. Merriam-Webster.com, s.v. "Incubus", accessed December 19, 2021, https://www.merriam-webster.com/dictionary/incubus?src=-search-dict-box.
2. Merriam-Webster.com, s.v. "Succubus", accessed December 19, 2021, https://www.merriam-webster.com/dictionary/succubus.
3. Genesis 1:27.
4. Revelation 12:9.
5. Revelation 13:2.
6. Genesis 5:3.

7. Flavius Josephus, The Antiquities of the Jews, 1.73, https://lexundria.com/j_aj/1.73/wst.
8. Washington Post article, "Artifacts Found In the Black Sea May Be Evidence of Biblical Flood" (Author, Guy Gugliotta, September 13, 2000).

CHAPTER FIFTEEN: ORDER IN CHAOS

1. Space.com, s.v. "planets and stars in the Milky Way Galaxy", accessed December 18, 2021, https://www.space.com/19103-milky-way-100-billion-planets.html.
2. Del Rio CM, White LJ. Separating spirituality from religiosity; A hylomorphic attitudinal perspective. Psychology of Religion Spirituality. Vol 4(2), May 2012, 123–142.
3. Sheldrake P. A Brief History of Spirituality. Somerset, NJ, USA: Wiley-Blackwell; 2007.
4. Aldwin CM, Park CL, Jeong Y-J, Nath R. Differing pathways between religiousness, spirituality, and health: a self-regulation perspective. Psychology of Religion Spirituality. 2014;6(1):9–21.
5. Resources.saylor.org, s.v. "Transatlantic slave trade", accessed November 2, 2015, https://resources.saylor.org/wwwresources/archived/site/wp-content/uploads/2011/04/Spain.pdf.
6. Digjamaica.com, s.v. "Kumina in Jamaica", accessed November 2, 2015, http://digjamaica.com/m/indigenous-religions-in-jamaica/kumina/.

CHAPTER SIXTEEN: KINGDOM OF DARKNESS ARMY RANKS

1. W. Nee, "The Importance of Authority," in Spiritual Authority (New York: Christian Fellowship Publishers, Inc., 1972): 10.
2. Ezekiel 28:14.
3. Luke 10:18.
4. Daniel 10:13.
5. "G746 - arche - Strong's Greek Lexicon (nkjv)." Blue Letter Bible. Web. 28 Dec, 2022. <https://www.blueletterbible.org/lexicon/g746/nkjv/tr/0-1/>.
6. Rick Renner, "Principalities, Powers, Rulers of Darkness, and Spiritual Wickedness", https://www.youtube.com/watch?v=JMfTGJFy0lo.
7. Ibid.

CHAPTER EIGHTEEN: A SOLITARY ACT

1. Mr. Magorium's Wonder Emporium. Directed by Zach Helm, written by

Zach Helm, performances by Dustin Hoffman, Natalie Portman, and Jason Bateman, 20th Century Fox, 2007.
2. 2 Corinthians 5:8.

CHAPTER NINETEEN: WHO SHALL SEPARATE US?
1. Mark 1:13; Revelation 11: 7, 13:1, 3, 4, 11, 12, 14, 15, 17, 18, 14:9, 11; 15:2; 16:2, 10, 13; 17:3, 7, 8, 11, 12, 13, 16; 17:17; 19:19, 20; 20:4, 10.
2. Ephesians 6:12.
3. Mark 9:21.
4. Matthew 18:19.
5. Ephesians 4:23.
6. Acts 20:28, Colossians 2:14.

CHAPTER TWENTY: WEAPONS OF WARFARE
1. 2 Timothy 2:25 (KJV).
2. For more in-depth teaching on repent, renounce, and break, please refer to the Cleansing Seminar by Timothy Davis, https://www.cleansingthechurch.com/cleansing-seminar.
3. Merriam-Webster.com, s.v. "Witness", accessed November 29, 2022, https://www.merriam-webster.com/dictionary/witness.
4. John 16:13-15 NET
5. Romans 5:5.
6. A. Murray, "The Spirit And the Blood," in The Blood of the Cross, (Whitaker House, 1981): 10-11.
7. Joel 2:23-29.
8. Isaiah 28:11-12.
9. Acts 2:17.
10. John 7:37-39.
11. John 3:8.
12. Acts 2:3.
13. 2 Corinthians 1:21-22.
14. 1 John 2:20.
15. Acts 2:3.
16. Daniel 3:27.
17. Isaiah 4:4.
18. Matthew 3:16.
19. Symbols of the Holy Spirit, s.v. "Holy Spirit Jack Hayford", accessed January

9, 2022, https://www.jackhayford.org/teaching/articles/symbols-of-the-holy-spirit/.
20. Andrew Murray, The Blood of the Cross, (Whitaker House, 1981), 17.
21. Andrew Murray, The Blood of the Cross, (Whitaker House, 1981), 11.
22. Leviticus 17:11, John 6:54, Hebrews 7:27.
23. 1 Peter 1:18-19, Acts 20:28, 2 Corinthians 5:17, Hebrews 9:12, Revelation 5:9, Hebrews 9:14, 2:14, 13:12; 1 John 3:8; 1 John 1:7.
24. Ephesians 1:7.
25. Hebrews 13:21.
26. Colossians 1:12-14, Isaiah 53:5, 1 Peter 2:24, Exodus 12.
27. Hebrews 9:14, 13:20.
28. Genesis 4:2-8, 10.
29. Greenwood, Norman N.; Earnshaw, Alan (1997). Chemistry of the Elements (2nd ed.), p. 620. Butterworth-Heinemann.
30. "Water, the Universal Solvent". U.S. Department of the Interior. usgs.gov (website). United States of America: USGS. October 22, 2019. Accessed December 15, 2020.
31. Reece, Jane B.; Urry, Lisa A.; Cain, Michael L.; Wasserman, Steven A.; Minorsky, Peter V.; Jackson, Robert B. (2013-11-10). Campbell Biology (10th ed.). Boston, Mass.: Pearson. p. 48.
32. Reece et al. 2013, p. 44.
33. Weingärtner, Hermann; Teermann, Ilka; Borchers, Ulrich; Balsaa, Peter; Lutze, Holger V.; Schmidt, Torsten C.; Franck, Ernst Ulrich; Wiegand, Gabriele; Dahmen, Nicolaus; Schwedt, Georg; Frimmel, Fritz H.; Gordalla, Birgit C. (2016). "Water, 1. Properties, Analysis, and Hydrological Cycle". Ullmann's Encyclopedia of Industrial Chemistry. Wiley-VCH Verlag GmbH & Co. KGaA. doi:10.1002/14356007.a28_001.pub3, p.2.
34. Britanica.com, s.v. "Holy water", accessed 12-27-21, https://www.britannica.com/topic/holy-water.
35. Exodus 29:4, 30:18-20, 40:12, 30-32.
36. Exodus 40:34-38.
37. "H6051 - anan - Strong's Hebrew Lexicon (nkjv)." Blue Letter Bible. Web. 22 Dec, 2022. <https://www.blueletterbible.org/lexicon/h6051/nkjv/wlc/0-1/>.
38. Exodus 7:19-20.
39. Exodus 14:21-29.
40. 1 Corinthians 10:1-4.
41. 1 Peter 3:20-21.

42. John 4:14, 7:38-39.
43. Revelation 22:1-2.
44. Ephesians 5:25-27..

CHAPTER TWENTY-ONE: LET'S BREAK SOME SOUL TIES!

1. To listen to the entire Pathway To Purity teaching, visit https://www.cleansingthechurch.com/product-page/the-pathway-to-purity.

CHAPTER TWENTY-TWO: CASTING OUT NEPHILIM

1. Hosea 4:6.
2. Genesis 6:11-12.
3. Genesis 6:8-9.
4. Luke 17:26.

CHAPTER TWENTY-THREE: FREEDOM FROM UNCLEAN SPIRITS

1. Matthew 12:43-45, Luke 11:24-26.
2. "G1831 - exerchomai - Strong's Greek Lexicon (nkjv)." Blue Letter Bible. Web. 29 Dec, 2022. <https://www.blueletterbible.org/lexicon/g1831/nkjnkjv/tr/0-1/>.
3. "G1544 - ekballo - Strong's Greek Lexicon (nkjv)." Blue Letter Bible. Web. 29 Dec, 2022. <https://www.blueletterbible.org/lexicon/g1544/nkjv/tr/0-1/>.
4. To purchase the ebook, visit https://www.amazon.com/UNCLEAN-SPIRITS-Satans-Best-Kept-Secrets-ebook/.
5. Mark 15:37; Luke 23:46.
6. Luke 16:22.

EPILOGUE: MY SECRET IS OUT!

1. Titus 2:14.

About the Author

DENISE DAVIS was born and raised in Hampton, Illinois, a tiny suburb of the Quad Cities. She left at age 19 to attend Life Pacific University in Los Angeles, California, where she made it home and raised her family for over 36 years.

Denise travels with her husband, Timothy, all over the world, speaking and ministering to hurting people. In 2020 they relocated back to the Quad Cities to be closer to her parents, which was a welcomed change. She divides her time between Hampton and Southern California, where she enjoys opportunities for intensive personal ministry.

She also writes, conducts research, and wears many hats to partner with Timothy in the cleansing ministry. She revitalizes herself through daily prayer and Bible study, taking trips to Mexico, Italy, England, Ireland, Scotland, Israel… well, just about anywhere, and snuggling up every day with her little white fluff ball of a puppy named Holly.

Denise and Timothy have six children and 18 grandchildren in four states, and make it a point to spend quality time with each of them every year.

For more information about
Denise Davis, visit her website at
www.doyousee.org
denisedavis@doyousee.org

Teachings by Timothy Davis Mentioned in this Book

The Cleansing Seminar
Alignment: Session One
Consecration: Session Two
Words: Session Three
Cleansing: Session Four
Pathway To Purity
Satan: The Fallen Cherub
Satan: The Flood
Unclean Spirits: One of Satan's Best-Kept Secrets
The Underworld

Where to Find Them

https://www.cleansingthechurch.com/store

Made in the USA
Middletown, DE
30 October 2023

41628269R00126